THE ECONOMIC FOUNDATIONS OF RISK MANAGEMENT

Theory, Practice, and Applications

THE ECONOMIC FOUNDATIONS OF RISK MANAGEMENT

Theory, Practice, and Applications

Robert Jarrow

Cornell

NEW JERSEY · LONDON · SINGAPORE · BEIJING · SHANGHAI · HONG KONG · TAIPEI · CHENNAI · TOKYO

Published by

World Scientific Publishing Co. Pte. Ltd.

5 Toh Tuck Link, Singapore 596224

USA office: 27 Warren Street, Suite 401-402, Hackensack, NJ 07601

UK office: 57 Shelton Street, Covent Garden, London WC2H 9HE

Library of Congress Cataloging-in-Publication Data

Names: Jarrow, Robert A., author.
Title: The economic foundations of risk management : theory, practice, and applications /
    Robert Jarrow (Cornell).
Description: New Jersey : World Scientific, [2016]
Identifiers: LCCN 2016033483| ISBN 9789813147515 (hc : alk. paper) |
    ISBN 9789813149960 (pbk : alk. paper)
Subjects: LCSH: Financial risk management. | Risk management--Economic aspects.
Classification: LCC HG173 .J337 2016 | DDC 658.15/5--dc23
LC record available at https://lccn.loc.gov/2016033483

British Library Cataloguing-in-Publication Data
A catalogue record for this book is available from the British Library.

Desk Editors: Anthony Alexander/Alisha Nguyen

Typeset by Stallion Press
Email: enquiries@stallionpress.com

Printed in Singapore

This book is dedicated to my family

Preface

In today's financial markets, risk management is based on models. The purpose of this book is to present the economics and not the mathematics of the models upon which current risk management practice is based. It is essential that any user of risk management models understands the assumptions underlying these models, the motivations for the assumptions, the benefits and the weaknesses of the structures. With this understanding, enlightened usage of these models is possible. Without this knowledge, risk management models are a black box, potentially a Pandora's box.

There are many books that emphasize the mathematics of risk management models. There are no books that emphasize the economic theory. This book fills this void. Consistent with this motivation, this book does not emphasize proofs, derivations, estimation, nor computations. Instead, mathematics is used as the language needed to explain risk management theory in a non-diluted and rigorous fashion.

This book is based on a set of lectures on risk management given at the Samuel Curtis Johnson Graduate School of Management, Cornell University.

About the Author

Robert Jarrow is a Professor at the Samuel Curtis Johnson Graduate School of Management, Cornell University and director of research at
Kamakura Corporation. He is the co-creator of the Heath–Jarrow–Morton
(HJM) model for pricing interest rate derivatives, the reduced form credit
risk model for pricing credit derivatives, and the forward price martingale
measure. These tools and models are now the standards used for pricing
and hedging derivatives in major investment and commercial banks. His
research was the first to study market manipulation using arbitrage-pricing
theory, and to distinguish forward/futures prices.

He has been the recipient of numerous prizes and awards including
the CBOE Pomerance Prize for Options Research, the Graham and Dodd
Scrolls Award, the Bernstein Fabozzi/Jacobs Levy Award, the 1997 IAFE/
SunGard Financial Engineer of the Year Award, and Risk Magazine's 2009
Lifetime Achievement Award. He is on the advisory board of *Mathematical
Finance* — a journal he co-started in 1989. He is also an associate or advisory editor for numerous other journals. He is an IAFE senior fellow, and
he is included in both the Fixed Income Analysts Society Hall of Fame and
the Risk Magazine's 50 member Hall of Fame. He has written six books,
including the first textbooks on the Black Scholes and the HJM models, as
well as over 200 publications in leading academic journals.

Contents

Part I

Introduction

Introduction

This book presents the economic foundations of risk management. It presents the theory, the practice, and applies this knowledge to provide a forensic analysis of some well-known risk management failures. By doing so, this book presents a unified framework for understanding how to manage the risk of an individual's or corporation's or financial institution's assets and liabilities. Providing a framework for analysis, understanding the underlying economics, is essential in practical risk management.

An individual or firm, financial or non-financial, owns a portfolio of assets and liabilities. This portfolio can be represented by a balance sheet that changes across time. Each asset and liability has a present value. For an asset this represents the cash received today if the asset is sold. For a liability this represents the cash paid today to retire the liability. The sum of the assets' less the liabilities' present values represents the individual's or firm's equity value. This is their net worth.

Assets and liabilities generate future cash flows, both positive and negative. As the future is uncertain, these future cash flows are also uncertain. They are random variables. As time passes, information about these future cash flows changes. This changing information changes the assets', liabilities', and equity's present values. We say that the prices of the assets, liabilities, and equity are a *stochastic process*. Alternatively stated, the prices of these quantities involve across time in a random fashion.

Since equity is the entity's net worth, if the value of equity declines then this is a loss. If the value of the equity increases, then this is a gain. Such random changes in value and cash flows across time have a variance, therefore the portfolio's changing equity value and cash flows entail "risk."

Individuals and firms utilize the cash flows from the portfolio to consume or to manage the firm's activities, respectively. They also buy/sell new assets and liabilities across time. The cash flows and changing balance sheet positions so obtained generate benefits or costs for these entities. The entities have preferences (likes/dislikes) over the different patterns of cash flows and balance sheet configurations obtained. It is natural, therefore, that rational entities will seek to maximize these preferences across time by managing the assets and liabilities in their portfolio - by managing the balance sheet. Managing this risk of an individual's portfolio or a firm's balance sheet is the topic of this book, called "risk management."

As alluded to in this description, there are four topics that need to be mastered in risk management. The first is to understand the assets and liabilities that trade. The second is to understand how to model the risks from holding the assets and liabilities. The third is to characterize an individual or firm's preferences. And, the fourth is to understand how to manage the risks of the traded assets and liabilities to maximize their preferences. These four topics compose the four parts of this book.

Part II

Traded Assets and Liabilities

Overview

To understand how to risk manage an entity's portfolio or balance sheet, we first need to understand what assets and liabilities are available for trading, and what are the characteristics of the markets within which they trade. Since one person's liability is another person's (the counter party's) asset, we really only need to understand the traded assets in an economy.

There are two basic types of assets: primary assets and derivatives. Derivatives are financial securities whose payoffs depend on the primary asset's payoffs and/or values. We discuss each of these in turn. The subsequent discussion is conceptual focusing on the economic considerations in trading assets. Institutional details are presented, but only in an abstract form so that the relevant economics of the institutional structures are understood.

.

Chapter 1

Primary Assets

This chapter discusses the primary assets. To understand the traded primary assets, the markets in which they trade need to be understood first.

1.1 Market Types

There are two types of markets in which assets trade: spot markets and forward markets.

By definition, a *spot market* is a market in which an asset is exchanged immediately for cash. An example of a spot market is a grocery store where one can buy oranges for cash.

By definition, a *forward market* is a market in which one agrees today, to buy an asset at a future (forward) date. Cash will be exchanged at the future date when the asset is delivered. An example of a forward market is an auto dealer who agrees to sell you a car which will be made in 2 months time at the auto factory. Delivery will take place immediately after production in 2 months. To trade in a forward market, a financial contract must be created and "signed" by both parties. This financial contract is an example of a derivative security. As such, we will discuss forward markets in the next Chapter. This chapter just concentrates on spot markets.

The structure of a spot market in which an asset trades can be different for different assets. From an economic point of view, the most important aspects of spot markets are the following three characteristics:

1. *Competitive or not.* Competitive means that the traders have no quantity impact from trading on the price of the asset purchased or sold. Hence, when trading they act as *price takers*. Any other market situation is defined to be non-competitive. An example of a non-

competitive market is one where buyers bargain with sellers over the price, and different buyers get different prices.

2. *Frictionless or not, and the type of frictions.* A frictionless market is a market without transaction costs and trading constraints. Transaction costs are fees paid to trade. Trading constraints include indivisibilities in the quantity of an asset traded, short sale restrictions, collateral/margin requirements, borrowing constraints, and bounds on quantities transacted. A frictionless market is the proverbial "ideal" market.

3. *Actively traded (large volume) or not.* This characteristic of a market often corresponds to liquid or illiquid markets. A *liquid market* is defined to be a competitive market where there is no quantity impact from trading on the price.

1.2   Asset Types

This section discusses the different types of assets that trade in spot markets. Notation for asset prices will be introduced. For the notation, we assume that the time horizon is given by $t \in [0, T]$. This is called a *finite horizon* model. Because the terminal date T can be quite large, say 10,000 years, finite horizon models are really without loss of generality. We impose the finite horizon assumption to simplify the mathematics.

There are two types of assets that trade in spot markets: physical commodities and financial securities.

1.2.1   Physical Commodities

Physical commodities that trade include currencies (U.S. dollars, Euros, etc.), precious metals (gold, silver, etc.), agricultural commodities (corn, wheat, etc.), energy related commodities (oil, gas, etc.), and so forth. Physical commodities also include residential housing and commercial properties. Physical commodities trade in different markets with respect to competition, frictions, and trading activity, e.g. gold versus residential housing. Gold markets are very competitive, with minimal frictions, and a large amount of trading activity. In contrast, residential housing markets contain many frictions. Houses are often unique. This makes buying and selling a house noncompetitive in the sense that few buyers are price takers. Housing buyers usually negotiate the terms of a transaction. In addition, residential housing markets contain frictions. There are large transaction costs often paid to realtors to help sell a house. Houses are sold in discrete units (it is very difficult to buy $1/3$ of a house). And, there are borrowing constraints when buying a house, because often substantial down payments are required as a percent of the purchase price.

The spot price of a physical commodity at time $t \in [0, T]$ will be denoted S_t.

1.2.2 Financial Securities

Various financial securities trade in spot markets that are considered primary assets. A *financial security* is a financial contract that obligates the issuer to pay certain cash flows at future dates and it may give the receiver ownership over specified physical assets at certain times or under certain events. A financial security is best understood by considering various examples that clarify the definition. The following partial list corresponds to financial securities discussed later in this book.

Common Stock

A corporation has a balance sheet. The corporation's assets minus its liabilities equal its equity, which is its net worth. The equity is publicly traded if ownership shares are issued against this equity and traded in financial markets. These ownership shares are called *common stock* or *equity*. They often pay regular dividends, perhaps quarterly. They sometime pay dividends by issuing additional (fractional) shares of stock called *stock dividends*. New shares can be issued by the corporation diluting the existing ownership claims or existing shares can be purchased by the corporation to increase ownership proportions, these are called *share issuances* or *repurchases*, respectively. Common stock trade in different international markets. Some markets are competitive and actively traded with minimal frictions, while some are not.

The notation for the time $t \in [0, T]$ price of a common stock will be S_t.

Zero-Coupon Bonds

Important in understanding the different interest rates are zero-coupon bonds. A *zero-coupon bond* is defined to be a financial security that promises to pay 1 dollar (the face value) at a future time period $\tau \leq T$ (the bond's maturity). To simplify the notation, and without loss of generality, we normalize the face value of the zero-coupon bond to be unity.

If the promised dollar is paid with probability one, then the zero-coupon bond is said to be *default-free*. Government debt of the U.S. and Germany are often believed to be default-free (in reality, nearly default-free). U.S.

and German default-free zero-coupon bonds trade with different maturities in competitive and actively traded markets with minimal frictions.

If the promised dollar may not be paid with positive probability, it is called a *risky zero-coupon bond*. Risky zero-coupon bonds are a hypothetical construct, they typically do not trade.

Consider a discrete time horizon $t = 0, 1, \ldots, T$.

Default-Free   The time t price of a zero-coupon bond paying a sure dollar at time τ is denoted $P(t, \tau)$ for $0 \le t \le \tau \le T$. Note that $P(t, t) = 1$ for all $t \in [0, T]$.

One particular zero-coupon bond is special at each time t. This is the bond maturing at time $t+1$. The return on this bond over $[t, t+1]$ is riskless since both the beginning and ending values are known for sure at time t. The return on this bond is called the *default-free spot rate of interest* or sometimes the *riskless rate*. It is

$$r_t \equiv r(t) \equiv \frac{1}{P(t, t+1)} - 1. \tag{1.1}$$

Another important interest rate is the implicit interest earned by the $\tau + 1$ maturity zero-coupon bond over the future time period $[\tau, \tau + 1]$. This is called the *time t forward rate for date τ* and denoted $f(t, \tau)$. More formally,

$$f(t, \tau) = \frac{P(t, \tau)}{P(t, \tau + 1)} - 1. \tag{1.2}$$

Note that $f(t, t) = r(t)$.

The yield on a zero-coupon bond corresponds to the "average" per period return earned on the zero-coupon bond if held until maturity. It is

$$y(t, \tau) = \frac{1}{\tau - t} \left[\frac{1}{P(t, \tau)} - 1 \right]. \tag{1.3}$$

Note that $y(t, t + 1) = r(t)$.

Risky   The time t price of a risky zero-coupon bond paying a promised dollar at time τ is denoted $D(t, \tau)$ for $0 \le t \le \tau \le T$. Analogous spot rates, forward rates, and yields on risky zero-coupon bonds can be defined. We do not need notation for these in the subsequent text.

Money Market Accounts

A money market account is a mutual fund that pays interest each period $t = 1, \ldots, T$ on invested funds. The mutual fund's asset pool is entirely invested in the shortest maturity zero-coupon bond available at each date.

If the mutual fund invests in default-free zero-coupon bonds, then it is a default-free money market account.

If it invests in risky zero-coupon bonds, then it is a risky money market account.

Default-Free The notation for the money market account's value across time is described as follows. We assume that a dollar is initially invested at time 0. By the definition of the money market account, over $[0,1]$ this dollar is invested in the default-free zero-coupon bond maturing at time 1, i.e. $P(0,1)$. It earns the default-free spot rate $r(0)$, see expression (1.1). At time 1, the initial dollar plus interest earned $[1 + r(0)]$ is invested in the zero-coupon bond maturing at time 2, i.e. $P(1,2)$. It earns the default-free spot rate $r(1)$ over $[1,2]$ and so forth for $t = 2, \cdots$.

We denote the time t value of a default-free money market account as B_t where

$$
\begin{aligned}
B_0 &= 1, \\
B_t &= B_{t-1}(1 + r(t-1)) = \prod_{i=0}^{t-1}(1 + r(i)).
\end{aligned}
\tag{1.4}
$$

Risky We will not need notation for a risky money market account's value.

Floating Rate Bond

A floating rate bond has a maturity $\tau \leq T$ and face value equal to 1 dollar. Setting the face value equal to 1 dollar is without loss of generality. A floating rate loan promises to pay interest at the end of every time period $t = 1, 2, \ldots, \tau$ and to pay the face value (principal) at time τ. The interest paid corresponds to the spot rate of interest (times the face value, which equals one). The loan is called *floating* because the spot rate changes (floats) across time and is not fixed. Note that since the face value is unity, the dollar payment equals the interest rate (a percentage).

If the promised payment is paid with probability one, the floating rate bond is default-free. In this case the interest paid is the default-free spot rate $r(t)$. For example, government debt of the U.S. is believed to be default-free (in reality, nearly default-free). The U.S. Treasury issues a floating rate bond.

If the promised payment does not occur with positive probability, it is a risky floating rate loan.

It is easy to see that after the interest is paid on a floating rate loan, the value of the floating rate loan resets and becomes equal to its face value.

Coupon Bonds

Coupon bonds are financial securities that promise to pay 1 dollar (the face value or principal) at a future time period $\tau \leq T$ (the maturity date). Over the intermediate time periods $t = 1, \ldots, \tau$ a coupon of $c > 0$ dollars is also promised to be paid. Note that since the face value is unity, this dollar coupon also equals the coupon rate (a percentage). Another name for a coupon bond is a *fixed rate loan*.

If the payments occur with probability one, then the coupon bond is default-free. For example, U.S. and German default-free coupon bonds trade with different maturities in competitive and actively traded markets with minimal frictions.

If there is a positive probability that a payment will not be paid, then the coupon bond is risky. Risky coupon bonds are issued by various corporations and governments world-wide. They usually trade in less competitive and less volume activity markets, with greater fictions than the markets in which U.S. and German government bonds trade.

Default-Free   The time t price of a default-free coupon bond with face value 1, coupon rate c, and maturity τ is denoted $\mathfrak{B}(t, \tau)$ for $0 \leq t \leq \tau \leq T$.

The time t yield $Y(t, \tau)$ on a default-free coupon-bond with face value 1, coupon rate c, and maturity τ is defined to be the solution to the following expression

$$\mathfrak{B}(t, \tau) = \sum_{i=1}^{\tau-t} \frac{c}{[1 + Y(t, \tau)]^i} + \frac{1}{[1 + Y(t, \tau)]^{\tau-t}}. \tag{1.5}$$

As before, this corresponds to the "average" per period return earned on the bond if held until maturity, but only if the coupon payments are reinvested at this same rate. It is the *internal rate of return* on the bond.

Risky   The time t price of a risky coupon bond with face value 1, coupon rate c, and maturity τ is denoted $\mathfrak{D}(t, \tau)$ for $0 \leq t \leq \tau \leq T$.

The time t yield $\mathcal{Y}(t, \tau)$ on a risky coupon-bond with face value 1, coupon rate c, and maturity τ is defined to be the solution to the following expression

$$\mathfrak{D}(t, \tau) = \sum_{i=1}^{\tau-t} \frac{c}{[1 + \mathcal{Y}(t, \tau)]^i} + \frac{1}{[1 + \mathcal{Y}(t, \tau)]^{\tau-t}}. \tag{1.6}$$

This corresponds to the "average" per period return earned on the bond if held until maturity, but only if the coupon payments are reinvested at this same rate *and the bond does not default on any promised payments.* It is the internal rate of return on the bond.

Foreign Currencies

Different currencies exist and spot exchange rates enable one to transfer one currency into another. For most currencies, currency exchange rate markets are competitive and actively traded with minimal frictions. They are noncompetitive when governments control or intervene to affect their domestic exchange rate.

The notation for dealing with foreign currencies is as follows. The domestic currency will always be termed "dollars." The foreign currency will always be called "f-dollars." The spot exchange rate at time $t \in [0, T]$ is the number of f-dollars that it takes to equal one dollar, denoted S_t. S_t is in units of f-dollars.

There is a term structure of f-dollar interest rates. For subsequent use, let $r_f(t)$ be the default-free spot rate in f-dollars.

1.3 Buying on Margin

Sometimes when one purchases an asset in the spot market, one can borrow from a second party - the *counter party* to the borrowing - part or all of the purchase price. This is called buying *spot on margin.* Borrowing to purchase an asset on margin is also called collateralized borrowing, where the asset purchased serves as the collateral for the loan. Collateralized borrowing is ubiquitous in financial markets.

The mechanism in which the borrowing occurs differs across spot markets. The maximum percent of the purchase price that can be borrowed differs across spot markets as well. For financial securities, margin is usually regulated by financial authorities and the market where the purchase is executed. For physical commodities, a bank or the seller might be the lender. As such, they determine the rules under which the borrowing takes place. These rules are called *margin requirements.*

Margin requirements are a type of trading constraint. One of the most important rules associated with margin requirements is a *margin call.* Usually, the value of the asset purchased must exceed a fixed percent of the borrowing over the life of the borrowing. If the value of the asset declines below this fixed percent, due to adverse market conditions, the borrower must supply more margin/collateral (perhaps in the form of cash or default-free securities) to reduce the value of the borrowing relative to the pledged assets. This call for more margin/collateral is the "margin call." If a margin call occurs, and the borrower is unable to provide the additional margin/collateral, then the borrower defaults on the borrowing.

1.4   Short Selling

Short selling is allowed in many markets. To short sell an asset, one needs to first borrow the asset from another person, promising to deliver the borrowed asset upon demand and any of the cash flows generated by the asset when borrowed. The short seller then sells the borrowed asset. This sale creates a cash inflow to the seller. The seller has the cash and a liability to the asset lender.

In financial markets, when one short sells an asset, the cash is usually held in an escrow account called a margin account, and the cash is not available to the short seller. In addition, more cash is usually required to be deposited in the margin account in case the borrowed asset increases in value. This additional cash is a security deposit intended to decrease the credit risk of the asset lender.

For physical commodities, the commodity lender determines the conditions under which the lending will occur (cash deposits, etc.). These will differ across lenders.

1.5   Asset Risks

There are four basic risks to buying and selling assets: market risk, credit risk, liquidity risk, and operational risk. There is a fifth risk, called funding risk, which is a conjunction of liquidity risk and the impact of trading constraints - borrowing limits, margin requirements, and/or collateral requirements. We discuss each of these risks in turn.

Market Risk

Market risk is defined to be the risk in buying and selling assets due to changing market prices in competitive and actively traded markets.

Credit Risk

Credit risk is defined to the risk that a counter party to a financial security (contract) will fail to perform on an obligation causing a financial loss. An example is a risky bond that defaults on its promised payments.

Liquidity Risk

Liquidity risk is the loss in value that may occur when trying to buy or sell an asset quickly. This is the contradiction of competitive and actively traded markets. This risk results from a quantity impact on the price from trading.

Operational Risk

Operational risk is the risk in buying and selling an asset caused by mismanagement, fraud, legal errors, or execution errors. If one views the buying and selling of an asset as a production process, then operational risk is the risk that an error occurs in the execution of a trade.

Funding Risk

When an entity (corporation, government, individual) enters financial distress, they often face funding risk. When in financial distress, *funding risk* is the inability to generate cash that is needed to forestall default and/or insolvency. *Insolvency* occurs when the value of an entity's liabilities exceeds the value of its assets. Alternatively stated, insolvency is when the value of an entity's equity reaches zero with losses generated for the liability holders.

Funding risk is the conjunction of liquidity risk and the impact of trading constraints, in particular borrowing limits and/or marginal requirements. To understand this interaction, imagine a bank that is in financial distress. In its daily operations, the bank is obligated to make cash payments to various counter parties due to numerous existing contracts. These cash payments could be employee salaries, interest payments on debt, or to meet margin calls. If it cannot meet these payments, it defaults on its contracts. The risk that it defaults is the entity's credit risk to its lenders.

When in financial distress, to raise cash to meet its cash flow obligations, the bank has two alternatives. One, is to borrow more. But in this case the trading constraints - borrowing limits/ margin requirements - become binding, and it cannot do so. Two, is to sell assets. But in this case the entity's liquidity risk has increased and the negative quantity impact on the price from asset sales creates difficulties. Indeed, if assets are sold to generate cash, the market price of the assets drop due to the sale, which causes margin calls to reoccur, creating a downward spiral. This inability to generate cash to meet cash payment obligations in financial distress is funding risk.

Chapter 2

Derivatives

A *derivative* is a financial security whose payoffs depend on the prices and cash flows of some primary assets or indexes created from the prices and cash flows of some primary assets. There exist derivatives on derivatives, or compound derivatives as well (by composition of payoffs, the original definition applies here too). Derivatives are a zero supply asset, i.e. for every buyer there is a seller of the derivative. The buyer and seller of a derivative are called the *counter parties*.

For this chapter we only consider derivatives where there is no counter party risk, i.e. the counter parties to the derivatives make the promised payments with probability one. We invoke this assumption to simplify the notation with respect to the payments made to the derivative's counter parties. This is nearly true in practice since both counter parties (in theory) provide sufficient collateral to guarantee the execution of all contracted payments.

2.1 The Four Basic Derivatives

There are four basic derivatives: forwards, futures, European calls, and European puts. If one understands the four basic derivatives, then one can understand all derivatives. Indeed, it can be shown that one can view the payoffs to any derivative as a limit of a combination of these four basic derivatives (see Carr and Madan [9]). To define a derivative, it is sufficient to give the derivative's payoffs for all times and states. This is the approach followed here. For a more complete reference on derivatives see Jarrow and Chatterjea [37].

2.1.1   Forwards

Consider a risky asset with time $t \in [0, T]$ price S_t.

A *forward contract* obligates the owner (long position) to buy the asset on the delivery date τ for a predetermined price. By market convention this price is set so that the value of the forward contract at initiation (time 0) is zero. This market clearing price is called the *forward price* and denoted $K(0, \tau)$. The time τ payoff to the forward contract is

$$[S_\tau - K(0, \tau)].$$

Note that this payoff can be positive or negative depending upon S_τ.

Forward Rate Agreements (FRAs)

A *forward rate agreement* is a forward contract on the default-free spot rate of interest. As such, it has a maturity τ, a FRA rate denoted a_τ, and a notional equal to one dollar. Setting the notional equal to unity is without loss of generality. The time τ payoff of the FRA per dollar notional is

$$[r(\tau - 1) - a_\tau].$$

Note that the spot rate in the payoff is that at time $\tau - 1$. One can think of this payoff as the difference in interests earned on the notional over the time period $[\tau - 1, \tau]$ and paid at time τ.

2.1.2   Futures

A *futures contract* is similar to, but different from, a forward contract. It is a financial contract, written on a risky asset S_t, with a fixed maturity τ. It represents the purchase of the asset at time τ via a *prearranged payment procedure*. The prearranged payment procedure is called *marking-to-market*. Marking-to-market obligates the purchaser (long position) to accept a cash flow stream equal to the changes in the futures prices for this contract over the time periods $t = 1, \cdots, \tau$.

The time t *futures prices*, denoted $k(t, \tau)$, are set (by market convention) such that newly issued futures contracts (at time t) on the same asset with the same maturity date τ have zero market value. Hence, futures contracts (by construction) have zero market value at all times, and a cash flow stream equal to $\triangle k(t, \tau) = k(t, \tau) - k(t - 1, \tau)$ at times $t = 1, \cdots, \tau$. At maturity, the last futures price must equal the asset's price $k(\tau, \tau) = S_\tau$.

Interest Rate Futures

An *interest rate futures* is a futures contract on the default-free spot rate of interest. As such, it has a maturity τ, a futures interest rate denoted $b(t,\tau)$ at times $t = 0, 1, \cdots, \tau$, and a notional equal to one dollar. Setting the notional equal to unity is without loss of generality. The cash flow stream equals $\triangle b(t,\tau) = b(t,\tau) - b(t-1,\tau)$ at times $t = 1, \cdots, \tau$. One can think of this as the differential interest earned on the dollar notional over the time period $[t-1,t]$ and paid at time t. At maturity, the last futures interest rate must equal the spot rate $b(\tau,\tau) = r(\tau)$.

2.1.3 European Puts

Consider a risky asset with time $t \in [0,T]$ price S_t.

A *European put option* has a maturity date τ and a strike price K. The option gives the right to sell the risky asset on the maturity date for K dollars. Its time τ payoff at maturity is

$$max[K - S_\tau, 0].$$

A European put option is equivalent to a term insurance policy insuring the risky asset for K dollars over the time period $[0,\tau]$.

An *American put option* allows one to sell the risky asset at any time over the option's life, not just at the maturity date.

Floorlet

A *floorlet* is a European put option written on the default-free spot rate of interest.

Consider a floorlet with maturity τ, strike k, and notional of 1 dollar. The time τ payoff to the floorlet is

$$max[k - r_{\tau-1}, 0].$$

Note that the spot rate is from time $\tau - 1$.

One can think of this as the differential interest earned on the notional over the time period $[\tau - 1, \tau]$ and paid at time τ, but only if it is positive.

A *floor* is a portfolio of floorlets.

2.1.4 European Calls

Consider a risky asset with time $t \in [0,T]$ price S_t.

A *European call option* has a maturity date τ and a strike price K. The option gives the right to buy the risky asset on the maturity date for K

dollars. Its time τ payoff at maturity is

$$max[S_\tau - K, 0].$$

An *American call option* allows one to buy the risky asset at any time over the option's life, not just at the maturity date.

Caplet

A *caplet* is a European call option written on the default-free spot rate of interest.

Consider a caplet with maturity τ, strike k, and notional of 1 dollar. The time τ payoff to the caplet is

$$max[r_{\tau-1} - k, 0].$$

Note that the spot rate is from time $\tau - 1$.

One can think of this as the differential interest earned on the notional over the time period $[\tau - 1, \tau]$ and paid at time τ, but only if it is positive.

A *cap* is a portfolio of caplets.

2.2   Notable Derivatives

To understand the case studies in Part VI of this book, we need to understand some notable derivatives trading in financial markets. As before we note that to define a derivative, it is sufficient to give the derivative's payoffs for all times and states. This is the approach followed below.

2.2.1   Repurchase Agreements (Repos)

Simply stated, a *repurchase agreement* is collateralized lending, using a bond as collateral. As collateralized lending, there is a term for the transaction and an interest rate paid, called the repurchase agreement or *repo rate*. Repurchase agreements can be used to facilitate the shorting of a bond, or leveraging the investment in the bond.

Let's consider a repurchase agreement on a coupon bond with time t price denoted $\mathfrak{B}(t)$ entered into at time 0 with a term of τ years and a repo rate of i_0. The cash flows from the repurchase agreement are as follows.

time	0	τ
cash flow	$-\mathfrak{B}(0)$	$+\mathfrak{B}(0)[1 + i_0]$
bond	*receive*	*deliver*

The counter party to a repurchase agreement is said to enter a *reverse repurchase agreement*. This is the same position with the signs of the cash flows reversed.

A repo can be used to facilitate shorting of the bond. Indeed, if one enters into a repurchase agreement, then one receives the bond as collateral. This bond can then be sold. Since the bond is not owned, this is shorting the bond. Here the borrowed bond is obtained via the repurchase agreement.

A reverse repo can also be used to lever a bond position, i.e. buying the bond and borrowing to do so. Leveraging via reverse repos takes place in the following manner.

1. Buy the bond.

2. Borrow the value of the bond using the bond as collateral (this is the reverse repo).

3. Take the cash obtained from the borrowing and purchase a second bond. This generates a leverage ratio of 2.

4. Next, borrow the value of the second bond using the second bond as collateral (this is a second reverse repo).

5. Take the cash obtained from the second borrowing and purchase a third bond. This gives a leverage ratio of 3.

6. Continue this process to obtain any desired leverage ratio.

2.2.2   Swaps

A swap is a financial contract where two counter parties agree to swap a pair of payments with respect to some notional regularly (e.g. every quarter) over some time horizon (e.g. five years). This section describes four different actively traded swaps.

Interest Rate Swaps

A *(plain vanilla) interest rate swap* has a swap rate c, a maturity date τ, and a notional of 1 dollar. Setting the notional equal to unity is without loss of generality.

Let's consider a *paying fixed, receiving floating* swap (receiving fixed, paying floating is the other side of the transaction). The swap holder pays c dollars and receives the spot rate of interest $r(t-1)$ at the end of every time period $t = 1, \cdots, \tau$. The notional is not exchanged at time 0 nor at time τ.

The swap's payoffs are:

time	0	1	$\cdots$	t	$\cdots$	τ
Swap		$[r_0 - c]$		$[r_{t-1} - c]$		$[r_{\tau-1} - c]$

By market convention, the swap rate c is set at time 0 so that the initial value of the swap is zero. Note that the payment at time t, $[r_{t-1} - c]$, can be viewed as the interest differential earned on the dollar notional over the time period $[t-1, t]$, which is paid at time t.

Equity Swaps

An *equity swap* has a fixed payment rate c, a maturity date τ, and a notional of 1 dollar. Setting the notional equal to unity is without loss of generality.

Let's consider a *pay fixed rate, receive index return* equity swap. The equity swap pays the fixed rate c and receives the return on an equity index $\frac{S_t - S_{t-1}}{S_{t-1}}$ at the end of every time period $t = 1, \cdots, \tau$. The notional is not exchanged at time 0 nor at time τ.

By market convention, the swap rate c is set at time 0 so that the initial value of the swap is zero.

FX Swaps

The currencies considered are dollars and f-dollars.

A *FX swap* has two interest rates $r(t), r_f(t)$ corresponding to the default-free spot rates in the two currencies, a maturity date τ, and two notionals: 1 dollar and S_0 f-dollars, where S_0 is the exchange rate f-dollars/dollars. Note that the time 0 notionals are equal in dollar value or f-dollar values.

Let's consider a *pay dollars and receive f-dollars* FX swap. The FX swap holder agrees to: (i) pay 1 dollar and receive S_0 f-dollars at time 0 (this is an exchange of notional), (ii) at the end of every time period $t = 1, \cdots, \tau$ pay floating $r_f(t)S_0$ f-dollars and receive $r(t)$ dollars (interest on the implicit loans), and (iii) at time τ, receive 1 dollar and pay S_0 f-dollars (return of the notional).

By construction, at time 0 this swap has zero value.

Credit Default Swaps (CDS)

A *credit default swap* is a term insurance policy issued on a risky coupon bond.

Consider both a risky and default-free coupon bond issued at time 0 with the same maturity date τ.

The default-free coupon bond has a coupon rate c, a maturity date τ, and a face value 1 dollar. Its time t price is denoted $\mathfrak{B}(t,\tau)$ for $0 \le t \le \tau \le T$.

The risky coupon bond has a coupon rate c_R, a maturity date τ, and a face value 1 dollar. Its time t price is denoted $\mathfrak{D}(t,\tau)$ for $0 \le t \le \tau \le T$.

Setting the face value equal to unity is without loss of generality.

Consider a CDS contract of maturity date $v \le \tau$ with notional 1 dollar written on the risky coupon bond $\mathfrak{D}(0,\tau)$ at time 0.

The CDS contract to the buyer is as follows (the CDS seller has the other side of this contract).

Starting at time 1 and continuing until time v, if no default occurs on the risky bond, the CDS pays the rate s per period.

In the event of default at time $\chi \le v$, the CDS pays s, it receives $\mathfrak{B}(\chi,\tau)$, and gives up $\mathfrak{D}(\chi,\tau)$. In this case, $\mathfrak{D}(\chi,\tau) < \mathfrak{B}(\chi,\tau)$ due to the lost coupon payments and the recovery rate on the risky coupon bond being less than 1.

If $\chi > v$, then the CDS contract expires at time v with no additional payments made after time v.

In reality the CDS receives the face value of the risky bond at χ, which is 1. We consider the hypothetical contract because in Chapter 13 it is shown that this is the contract needed to synthetically construct a default-free coupon bond from a risky coupon bond.

The payoffs of a CDS with maturity v, if default happens at time χ, are given by the following:

time	0	1	$\cdots$	$\chi - 1$	χ	$\cdots$	v
CDS		$-s$		$-s$	$-s + \mathfrak{B}(\chi,\tau) - \mathfrak{D}(\chi,\tau)$	0	0

Let C_0 denote the value of the CDS at time 0. By market convention, the CDS rate s is that rate which sets $C_0 = 0$.

2.2.3 Swaptions

A *swaption* is an option on an interest rate swap.

Let's consider a *paying fixed, receiving floating* interest rate swap with swap rate c, maturity date τ, and notional of 1 dollar. Let its time t value be denoted C_t.

Consider a European call option on this swap with maturity $\chi < \tau$ and strike price K. The payoff to this swaption at its maturity date χ is

$$max[C_\chi - K, 0].$$

We note that this is a compound derivative, i.e. a derivative (call option) on another derivative (swap).

2.2.4   Bonds with Embedded Options

Risky bonds trade with various embedded options in their debt contracts. Two common embedded options are convertible provisions and callable provisions.

A *callable bond* is a risky coupon bond where the issuer of the bond has the right to call back (retire the bond) by paying a predetermined price. The predetermined price can depend on the date it is paid. These bonds often have lockout periods early in the bond's life where the bond cannot be called.

A callable bond is equivalent to an ordinary risky coupon bond plus a short position in an American call option with the strike price equal to the call price.

A *convertible bond* is a risky coupon bond issued by a corporation where the holder of the bond has the right (option), usually after an initial lock out period, to convert the bond into a fixed number of equity shares of the corporation.

A convertible bond is equivalent to an ordinary risky coupon bond plus being long a call option on the corporation's equity with the strike price equalling the value of the underlying (ordinary) bond.

2.2.5   Inverse Floaters

For the purposes of this description, we first assume that the issuer of the inverse floater is default-free.

An inverse floater is a fixed income security with a maturity date τ, a notional of 1 dollar (without loss of generality), and a coupon rate of c. Its coupon payments are reduced as an underlying floating rate increases (this is the inverse floating aspect).

Let r_t denote the default-free spot rate of interest.

The inverse floater is defined by the following cash flows.

time	0	1	2	...	τ
inverse floater		$max[c - r_0, 0]$	$max[c - r_1, 0]$	...	$max[c - r_{\tau-1}, 0] + 1$

At each date t over the fixed income security's life, the buyer of the inverse floater receives the fixed coupon rate less the spot rate (times the notional), but only if the difference is positive. The 1 dollar notional is paid at time τ.

Given this description, we can now relax the default-free assumption on the issuer. In this case the cash flows are only promised, and not for sure. Hence, default is possible. In addition, the floating rate is not the default-free spot rate, but the relevant credit-risky spot rate of interest for the issuer of the inverse floater.

2.2.6 Asset Backed Securities

This section discusses *asset-backed securities* (ABS), sometimes called structured debt. A special case of ABS are *collateralized debt obligations* (CDOs). They differ only in the assets held in their collateral pools. ABS hold untraded loans in their collateral pools while CDOs hold traded ABS bonds. The distinction will become clear once the definitions are provided.

An ABS is best understood as a liability issued by a firm or corporation, although the legal structure of the entity issuing an ABS is quite different from a typical corporation, usually a special purpose vehicle (SPV). A firm's balance sheet consists of assets, liabilities, and equity.

The assets purchased by an SPV are called the *collateral pool*. It is the collateral underlying the SPV's liabilities. The collateral pool usually consists of a collection of loans of a particular type, for example, either auto loans, student loans, credit card loans, commercial real estate loans, or residential mortgages.

To help finance the purchase of the collateral pool, the SPV issues debt. These liabilities issued by the SPVs are the ABS. In the case where the collateral pool consists of mortgages, these are sometimes RMBS (*residential mortgage backed securities*).

The debt is issued in various tranches or slices, from the senior bond tranches to the mezzanine to the junior bond tranches. These bond tranches have different claims to both the cash flows from the collateral pool and any losses realized on the collateral pool.

The cash flows from the collateral pool, consisting of interest and principal payments, are paid to the most senior bonds first, then the mezzanine bonds, then the junior bonds, with the residual going to the equity (see Exhibit 1). The cash flow and loss allocations across the various bond tranches is called the *waterfall*. The losses are realized in the reverse order, starting with the equity first, moving to the junior, the mezzanine, then the senior bond tranches. As such, the senior bond tranches are the safest with respect to default risk, while the equity are the riskiest securities in this regard.

Assets	Liabilities	Waterfall
	senior bond tranches	
	mezzanine bond tranches	
collateral pool	junior bond tranches	cash flows ↓ losses ↑
	Equity	

Exhibit 1: The Cash Flow and Loss Waterfalls to an ABS

Part III

Modeling Risks

Overview

To manage risks, we need to be able to quantify the risks. This means modeling. For risk management we are interested in determining present values and how present values change across time. There are two market based approaches for determining present values: no-arbitrage and equilibrium. Both determine an asset's present value by using the market's *state price density*.

State Price Density

To define the market's state price density, consider a security paying a dollar only at time $t \in [0, T]$ in state $\omega \in \Omega$, denoted $1_{\{t,\omega\}}$. This is sometimes called an indicator function. Informally, the present value of this dollar paid at time t in state ω is obtained by computing its *certainty equivalent*, discounting, and then multiplying by the probability that state ω occurs, i.e. $\frac{Y_t(\omega)}{B_t(\omega)} p(\omega)$ where $Y_t(\omega)$ is the certainty equivalent of a dollar paid at time t in state ω, $B_t(\omega)$ is the discount factor, and $p(\omega)$ is the probability of state ω. A certainty equivalent is the dollar amount that one would be indifferent between taking this amount for sure at time t in state ω or realizing the risky payoff $1_{\{t,\omega\}}$ instead.

The *state price density* is defined to be $\frac{Y_t(\omega)}{B_t(\omega)}$, which corresponds to the discounted certainty equivalent at time t in state ω. State price densities are sufficient to determine an asset's present value. Indeed, to get the present value of any asset paying $S_t(\omega)$ at time t in state ω, which corresponds to the magnitude of dollars paid at time t in state ω, simply sum the present value of these payoffs across all possible states, i.e. $\sum_{\omega \in \Omega} S_t(\omega) \frac{Y_t(\omega)}{B_t(\omega)} p(\omega)$. In this manner, any asset's present value can be determined.

No-arbitrage versus Equilibrium Models

A model is characterized by its assumptions. We now describe the assumptions underlying the standard no-arbitrage and equilibrium models. Both no-arbitrage and equilibrium models assume that the economy is frictionless and competitive. *Frictionless* means that there are no transactions costs and no trading constraints, e.g. short sale constraints or margin requirements. *Competitive* means that all traders act as price takers, believing that their trades have no quantity impact on the price.

In addition, no-arbitrage models assume that the economy has no arbitrage opportunities (this term will be defined later in the text). The assumption of no arbitrage opportunities is a mild assumption, being satisfied in most markets. In contrast, equilibrium models impose additional assumptions on traders' preferences, endowments, and the market clearing mechanism. These additional assumptions imply as a consequence that there will be no arbitrage opportunities in the economy. Hence, equilibrium models are a subset of no-arbitrage models.

Unfortunately, the additional equilibrium model assumptions are controversial with respect to their validity in financial markets. Disagreement exists in the academic literature concerning traders' preferences: are they rational or not (this topic is debated in the behavioral finance literature)? Disagreement also exists in the academic literature with respect to the market clearing mechanism: a Nash equilibrium or supply equal to optimal demands (this topic is debated in the market microstructure literature). If the incorrect structures are assumed, then the equilibrium model is misspecified and its predictions invalid. Constructing an equilibrium model that matches market realities is a difficult task.

For this reason, no-arbitrage models are more robust than equilibrium models. Consequently, they are more useful in practice because less assumptions means that no-arbitrage models apply in more circumstances. Less assumptions, however, also imply that less can be said about the asset's state price density. As will be shown later in this book, no-arbitrage guarantees the existence of a state price density that satisfies certain properties. Identifying the state price density in a no-arbitrage model involves using market data and empirical methods. In contrast, equilibrium models give a unique characterization of the state price density in terms of trader's preferences and the economy's aggregate consumption process. Although conceptually pleasing, this additional characterization is less useful in practice because preferences are unobservable and as mentioned above, subject to considerable controversy.

Uses of No-arbitrage Models

For the remainder of the book, we use no-arbitrage models to quantify present values. No proofs will be given for quoted theorems, we only explain the economic meaning and importance of the relevant theorems. References are provided for all proofs. As will become evident, no-arbitrage models are used in two important ways.

1. To find arbitrage opportunities for trading purposes, and

2. given no-arbitrage prices, to risk manage a portfolio, i.e. to change a portfolio's risk profile by hedging various risks.

Both uses will be discussed in subsequent Chapters.

Chapter 3

Market Risk (Equities, FX, Commodities)

This chapter introduces the no-arbitrage models for pricing market risk, assuming that default-free interest rates are non-random. This constant interest rate assumption restricts the model's use to assets that are short-dated and whose price movements are uncorrelated to interest rates. Hence, the qualification in the chapter title to equities, foreign currencies (FX), and commodities. For real applications, since interest rates are stochastic, the assumption of constant interest rates needs to be relaxed. This will be done in the next chapter.

Historically, the no-arbitrage approach for pricing assets under constant interest rates was first presented by Black Scholes Merton (BSM) [5], [52] in the context of a very simple evolution for the risky asset price process, called geometric Brownian motion. For the purposes of this chapter, although we maintain the constant interest rate assumption, we generalize the evolution of the asset price process. Because the model presented here is based on the original BSM paper, we call it the BSM methodology.

3.1   Set up

To characterize the randomness in the economy, we consider a continuous time and finite time horizon $[0, T]$ model. The uncertainty in the economy is captured by a filtered probability space satisfying the usual conditions $(\Omega, \mathcal{F}, (\mathcal{F}_t), \mathbb{P})$, see Protter [56]. In this collection, Ω is the state space representing the possible states $\omega \in \Omega$ in the economy over $[0, T]$. The set $\mathcal{F}$ is a σ- algebra. This is the set of events (collections of states) over which probabilities are defined. The information flows over time are captured by the filtration $(\mathcal{F}_t)_{t \in [0,T]}$, which is an increasing sequence of σ-algebras with $\mathcal{F}_T = \mathcal{F}$. And finally, the likelihoods of the events in $\mathcal{F}$ are given by the *statistical* probability (measure) $\mathbb{P}$. By "statistical" is meant that this probability governs which states are realized and reflected in historical data, so that statistical methods can be used to infer the generating probability $\mathbb{P}$.

The BSM methodology is characterized by the following additional assumptions.

Frictionless and competitive markets.

Frictionless means that there are no transactions costs and no trading constraints, e.g. borrowing constraints, short sale constraints, or margin requirements. Competitive means that all traders act as price takers, believing that their trades have no quantity impact on the price.

No interest rate risk.

Traded is a money market account with initial value $B_0 = 1$ and time t value

$$B_t = e^{rt} \tag{3.1}$$

where r, the default-free spot rate of interest, is a constant.

Risky asset price evolution.

Traded is a risky asset whose market price at time t is denoted S_t. We assume that $S > 0$, that the risky asset has no cash flows, and that

$$S_t = S_0 + \int_0^t \mu_S(u)du + \int_0^t \sigma_S(u)dL(u) \tag{3.2}$$

where $L(t)$ is a Brownian motion under $\mathbb{P}$, capturing the randomness in the evolution of the asset price process with $L(0) = 0$, and where μ_S, σ_S are very general stochastic processes, depending upon the state of the economy. The restrictions imposed on μ_S, σ_S are those needed to make this expression well-defined as a stochastic integral (see Protter [56] for the definition of a stochastic integral).

We can understand this expression by considering a small time interval $[t, t + \Delta t]$. Over this time interval, expression (3.2) can be approximated by

$$\triangle S_t = \mu_S(t)\triangle t + \sigma_S(t)\triangle L(t) \tag{3.3}$$

where $\triangle S_t = S_{t+\triangle t} - S_t$ and $\triangle L(t) = L(t + \triangle t) - L(t)$. Here, the change in the asset's price is decomposed into (i) a random shock $\triangle L(t)$, which is normally distributed, scaled by the *asset's volatility* $\sigma_S(t)$, plus (ii) an expected change that is proportional to the time interval $\mu_S(t)\triangle t$, called the *drift*.

The assumption of no cash flows on the risky asset is for simplicity of the presentation and can easily be relaxed. The assumption of only one risky asset is also for simplicity and can easily be extended to many traded risky assets.

Definition 3.1. A *trading strategy* with initial wealth x is defined to be a specification of the holdings in the money market account and risky asset, $(\alpha_B(t), \alpha_S(t))$ for all t and ω that is *predictable* with respect to $(\mathcal{F}_t)$. Predictable means that the trading strategy can only depend on information from the past and the present (in a left-continuous manner), see Protter [56].

The time t value of this trading strategy is given by

$$X_t = \alpha_B(t)B_t + \alpha_S(t)S_t \qquad (3.4)$$

with $X_0 = x$.

Definition 3.2. The trading strategy $(\alpha_B(t), \alpha_S(t))$ with value process X_t is said to be *self-financing* if

$$X_t = x + \int_0^t [\alpha_B(u)dB_u + \alpha_S(u)dS_u]. \qquad (3.5)$$

Over a small time interval $[t, t+\triangle t]$, this expression can be approximated by

$$\triangle X_t = \alpha_B(t)\triangle B_t + \alpha_S(t)\triangle S_t \qquad (3.6)$$

where $\triangle B_t = B_{t+\triangle t} - B_t$.

This condition requires that the change in the trading strategy's time t value is just the accumulated gains and losses on the portfolio, with no cash inflows or outflows. Hence, this explains the meaning of the phrase self-financing.

Continuous time models enable the investor to trade an infinite number of times in any finite interval. Because of this ability, a trading strategy analogous to a *doubling strategy* in gambling can be constructed.

Example. *(Doubling Strategy)*

A typical doubling strategy can be constructed by considering betting on the outcome, say heads, of the flip of a fair coin.

The player bets $1 on the first flip. If the flip is heads, the player wins $1 and ends the game. If the flip is tails, the player loses $1.

Suppose the flip is tails, then a doubling strategy is for the player to continue playing and to bet $2 = 2 × $1 on the next flip. If heads, she wins $2. This covers her $1 loss on the previous bet, she wins $1 in total, and ends the game. If tails, she loses $2. Her total losses are now $3.

If tails, the player continues playing and she bets $4 = 2 × $2 on the next flip. If tails she wins $4. This covers her total losses of $3, and she wins $1 in total, and ends the game. If tails, she continues doubling her bets .... .

The interesting fact about a doubling strategy is that if the player can gamble an infinite number of times, like in a continuous trading model, a heads will eventually occur. The trader will win $1 for sure by playing this game. Hence, a doubling strategy creates a sure dollar from nothing (zero initial investment).

In reality, of course, such trading strategy's are infeasible due to limits on the ability of any player in the above game to get credit if a large losing streak occurs. Who would be willing to lend her more cash so that she can continue playing the game if her losses were enormous, say $100 million dollars? No one, because with probability 0.5 she may lose again on the next flip and not be able to repay the borrowings (unless she can borrow again, and again, and again until she eventually wins).

This ends the example.

To exclude doubling strategies in our continuous time model, analogous to the above example, we add an implicit credit constraint on borrowing. This is done by only considering trading strategies whose values (losses) do not fall below some uniform lower bound. Formally, we consider the following restricted class of trading strategies.

Definition 3.3. A self-financing trading strategy $(\alpha_B(t), \alpha_S(t))$ with value process X_t is said to be *admissible* if there exists a constant $\delta > 0$ such that $X_t \geq -\delta$ for all t with probability one.

Given this, we can now define the proverbial "free lunch," which is called an arbitrage opportunity.

Definition 3.4. An *arbitrage opportunity* is defined to be any admissible self-financing trading strategy $(\alpha_B(t), \alpha_S(t))$ with value process X_t such that

$$
\begin{array}{ccc}
X_0 = 0 & | & | \quad X_0 = x < 0 \\
\mathbb{P}(X_T \geq 0) = 1 & | \quad \text{or} \quad | & \mathbb{P}(X_T = 0) = 1 \\
\mathbb{P}(X_T > 0) > 0 & | & |
\end{array}
\qquad (3.7)
$$

An arbitrage opportunity is one of two types of self-financing trading strategies. The first is where no cash is invested, it generates a non-negative payoff for sure at time T, and a strictly positive payoff at time T with positive probability. This is analogous to receiving a free gift of a lottery ticket for a future lottery. The second is where cash is received (it is a liability) at time 0 and the liability disappears at a future date T with probability one. This is analogous to receiving a free gift of a dollar bill. Hence, an arbitrage opportunity is a desirable trading strategy.

We assume that no-arbitrage is satisfied by the evolution in expression (3.3). In continuous time we need to strengthen this assumption to also exclude approximate arbitrage opportunities. This stronger "no approximate" arbitrage assumption is called *No Free Lunch with Vanishing Risk* (NFLVR). Because NFLVR is a technical definition involving the notion of limits, we exclude a formal statement (see Jarrow and Protter [42] for this definition). Nonetheless, this additional strengthening of the no arbitrage assumption is needed for the subsequent theory, and we necessarily assume that the evolution in expression (3.3) satisfies NFLVR.

To price derivatives we need to impose one additional assumption. This assumption requires a definition.

Definition 3.5. The risky asset S_t is undominated, it satisfies *no dominance* (ND), if there is no admissible self-financing trading strategy $(\alpha_B(t), \alpha_S(t))$ with value process X_t and initial wealth x such that

$$
x = S_0
$$
$$
\mathbb{P}(X_T \geq S_T) = 1
$$
$$
\mathbb{P}(X_T > S_T) > 0.
$$

The definition of no dominance states that there is no self-financing trading strategy that has the same initial cost as the risky asset, but always generates a value at time T at least as large as the value of the risky asset, and sometimes a strictly greater value. Of course, if the risky asset is dominated, no one would want to just buy and hold the risky asset. If anyone desired the payoff to the risky asset, they would hold the dominating self-financing trading strategy instead to obtain the same payoff but at a lower cost. Consequently, the existence of a dominated risky asset is inconsistent with the well-functioning of a financial market. We also assume that ND holds for the evolution given in expression (3.3).

3.2   Results

We are now ready to state our first result. Before stating our first result, however, we need to introduce some terminology from probability theory (for formal definitions involving measurability conditions see Protter [56]). Consider a stochastic process Z_t.

We say that Z_t is a *martingale under the probability* $\mathbb{P}$ if $Z_t = E^{\mathbb{P}}\left(Z_T \mid \mathcal{F}_t\right)$ and $Z_t = E^{\mathbb{P}}\left(|X_t|\right) < \infty$ for all $t \in [0, T]$.

Martingales represent "fair games" in probability theory because the current value of the process equals its expected future value. Hence, because they represent "fair games," they will play an important role in the theory presented below.

We say that Z_t is a *local martingale under the probability* $\mathbb{P}$ if there exists a sequence of stopping times $\lim_{n \to \infty} \tau_n = \infty$ for sure such that $Z_{min(t, \tau_n)}$ is a martingale for all $n = 1, \ldots, \infty$. A *stopping time* τ_n is a random future time whose realization (or non-realization) is known at each time $t \in [0, T]$.

Local-martingales are a generalization of martingales. They are stochastic processes that are martingales on a sequence of stopping times. Although technical in appearance, local-martingales are the stochastic processes generated by the values of admissible self-financing trading strategies. Consequently, they also play an important role in the subsequent theory.

Our first theorem is known as the first fundamental theorem of asset pricing.

Theorem 3.6. *(First Fundamental Theorem of Asset Pricing)*
   The market satisfies NFLVR if and only if there exists a probability $\mathbb{Q}$ equivalent to $\mathbb{P}$ such that $\frac{S_t}{B_t}$ is a local martingale.

For a proof see Delbaen and Schachermayer [15].

The probability $\mathbb{Q}$ in this theorem is called a *local martingale probability.* "Equivalent" means that the two probabilities $\mathbb{Q}$ and $\mathbb{P}$ agree on zero probability events.

This theorem states that the market satisfies NFLVR (no approximate arbitrage opportunities) if and only if there exists a probability $\mathbb{Q}$ equivalent to $\mathbb{P}$ such that the normalized risky asset price process $\frac{S_t}{B_t}$ is a $\mathbb{Q}$ local martingale. This theorem is important because it transforms an economic notion (NFLVR) into a mathematical condition for the normalized risky asset price process. The economic interpretation of this theorem will follow later in this Chapter.

Let the payoff to a derivative $C_T \geq 0$ be nonnegative and $\mathcal{F}_T$ - measurable. $\mathcal{F}_T$−measurable means that the payoff only depends on the information available at time T. These C_T represent the set of all possible nonnegative random variables at time T, i.e. it is the set of all possible derivatives' payoffs; denote it $\mathcal{L}_+^0$.

Definition 3.7. Suppose the market satisfies NFLVR. Let $\mathbb{Q}$ be an equivalent local martingale probability. The market is *complete* (with respect to $\mathbb{Q}$) if for all $C_T \in \mathcal{L}_+^0$ such that $E^{\mathbb{Q}}\left(\frac{C_T}{B_T}\right) < \infty$, there exists an admissible self-financing trading strategy $(\alpha_B(t), \alpha_S(t))$ with initial value x and time t value $X_t = \alpha_B(t)B_t + \alpha_S(t)S_t$ such that $\frac{X_t}{B_t} = E^{\mathbb{Q}}\left(\frac{C_T}{B_T}|\mathcal{F}_t\right)$ for all $t \in [0, T]$.

First, note that the definition of a complete market implies that the admissible self-financing trading strategy satisfies $X_T = C_T$. Thus, given any derivative's payoff, in a complete market an admissible self-financing trading strategy exists that matches its time T payoffs. Furthermore, the value of the admissible self-financing trading strategy, normalized by the money market account's value, is a $\mathbb{Q}$ martingale. This observation will prove useful below. We can now state the second fundamental theorem of asset pricing.

Theorem 3.8. *(Second Fundamental Theorem of Asset Pricing)*
   Given NFLVR,
   the market is complete if and only if the equivalent martingale probability $\mathbb{Q}$ *is unique.*

For a proof see Harrison and Pliska [22].

This theorem states that under NFLVR (i.e., there exists of an equivalent local martingale probability), the market is complete if and only if the martingale probability is unique. Note that we do not need the market to satisfy ND for either of these two theorems. The next theorem characterizes the importance of assuming the market satisfies ND.

Theorem 3.9. *(Third Fundamental Theorem of Asset Pricing)*
   The market satisfies NFLVR and ND if and only if there exists a probability $\mathbb{Q}$ *equivalent to* $\mathbb{P}$ *such that*

$$S_t = E^{\mathbb{Q}}\left(\frac{S_T}{B_T}|\mathcal{F}_t\right)B_t \qquad \text{for all } t. \qquad (3.8)$$

For a proof see Jarrow and Larsson [38].
   This theorem states that the normalized risky asset price process $\frac{S_t}{B_t}$ is a $\mathbb{Q}$ martingale if and only if the market satisfies NFLVR and ND. Hence,

ND is required to insure that $\frac{S_t}{B_t}$ is a $\mathbb{Q}$ martingale, and not just a $\mathbb{Q}$ local martingale. The difference between these two conditions is related to the existence of an asset price bubble, which will be discussed below.

$\mathbb{Q}$ is called a *risk-neutral probability* or a *martingale probability*. It is called a risk-neutral probability because expression (3.8) is how one would compute the present value of the risky asset's time T payout in a world populated by risk neutral investors each with the probability beliefs given by $\mathbb{Q}$. We emphasize that this is only a "name" because investors are not risk neutral, they are most likely risk averse, and their beliefs are given by $\mathbb{P}$ and not $\mathbb{Q}$.

As already noted, this theorem gives a formula for computing the present value of the asset's time T payoff. Alternatively stated, this theorem gives conditions under which there exists a state price density. The state price density is given by the expression $\frac{Y_t(\omega)}{B_t} \equiv \frac{E^{\mathbb{Q}}\left(\frac{d\mathbb{Q}}{d\mathbb{P}}|\mathcal{F}_t\right)(\omega)}{B_t}$ where the numerator corresponds to the certainty equivalent of a dollar paid at time t in state ω and the denominator corresponds to the discount factor.

This present value represents the value paid to buy the asset if after purchase, one has to hold the asset forever and never resell. Consequently, it is also called the asset's *fundamental value*. Under this interpretation, this theorem characterizes the conditions under which the asset's fundamental and market prices are equal. We will return to this observation below when discussing bubbles.

Before concluding this section, we note that assuming an asset's price evolution as given in expression (3.3) is a very strong assumption. The restrictions imposed on the evolution's drift and volatility (μ_S, σ_S) imply whether: (i) NFLVR holds or not, (ii) ND holds or not, and (iii) the market is complete or not. As discussed above, the BSM methodology requires structure sufficient to imply NFLVR and ND, so only those evolutions are considered. We now discuss the importance of assuming that the market is complete.

3.3   Pricing

Assuming that the market satisfies NFLVR, ND, and is complete, one can show that the price of any derivative satisfies *risk-neutral valuation*.

Theorem 3.10. *(Risk-Neutral Valuation of Derivatives)*
Let the market satisfy NFLVR, ND, and be complete.
Let $\mathbb{Q}$ be the risk-neutral probability.
Then, given $C_T \in \mathcal{L}^0_+$ with $E^{\mathbb{Q}}\left(\frac{C_T}{B_T}\right) < \infty$,

$$C_t = E^{\mathbb{Q}}\left(\frac{C_T}{B_T} \mid \mathcal{F}_t\right) B_t \qquad \text{for all } t. \qquad (3.9)$$

For a proof see Jarrow [32].

As with the terminology risk-neutral probability, this expression is called *risk-neutral valuation* because it represents the equilibrium value the derivative would have in a world consisting of risk neutral investors each with the probability beliefs given by $\mathbb{Q}$. We emphasize that this is only a "name" because investors are not risk neutral, they are most likely risk averse, and their beliefs are given by $\mathbb{P}$ and not $\mathbb{Q}$.

Although expression (3.9) is written abstractly, computing this derivative's time t price is equivalent to evaluating the expectation on the right side of this expression. Computing this expectation is an easy exercise given the evolution of the risky asset price process as in expression (3.2). Often, an analytic formula is available, e.g. the BSM call option formula. If no analytic formula is known, then simulation always works (see Glasserman [20]).

In a complete market, if any derivative does not satisfy expression (3.9), then there is a trading opportunity - either an FLVR or a dominated security. In either case, trading profits are available. This illustrates one use of a no-arbitrage pricing model - pricing.

3.4 Synthetic Construction

The proof of Theorem 3.10's logic is as follows. First, given a derivative $C_T \in \mathcal{L}^0_+$ with $E^{\mathbb{Q}}\left(\frac{C_T}{B_T}\right) < \infty$ where $\mathbb{Q}$ is the risk-neutral probability, since the market is complete we know that there exists an admissible self-financing trading strategy $(\alpha_B(t), \alpha_S(t))$ that generates the derivative's payoffs, i.e. $C_T = X_T$. Using expression (3.4) on the time t value of this trading strategy, X_t, in conjunction with expression (3.8), yields expression (3.9). Here the initial value of the admissible self-financing trading strategy $X_0 = x$ represents the cost of constructing the derivative synthetically. Hence, the arbitrage free price for the derivative must be $x = C_0$.

As noted in the proof's logic, at any time t we have that:

$$C_t = X_t = \alpha_B(t)B_t + \alpha_S(t)S_t. \qquad (3.10)$$

This implies that to synthetically construct the derivative security's change in value over $[t, t + \triangle t]$, the number of units of the money market account must be $\alpha_B(t)$ and the number of shares of the risky asset must be $\alpha_S(t)$. The number of shares in the risky asset used to replicate the derivative's change in value is called the *hedge ratio*. To get $(\alpha_B(t), \alpha_S(t))$, one takes the partial derivatives of the formula for C_t with respect to (B_t, S_t).

This synthetic construction is the basis of the local risk management methods discussed in Part V below. This illustrates the second use of a no-arbitrage model - hedging or risk management.

If the market is incomplete, then one cannot synthetically construct an arbitrary derivative $C_T \in \mathcal{L}_+^0$. In addition, the risk-neutral probability $\mathbb{Q}$ is not unique and one cannot uniquely price derivatives, i.e. more than one price exists for expression (3.9). In this case, to hedge a derivative, one must employ other derivatives that trade. Consequently, risk management in an incomplete market is more difficult. For this reason most models used in risk management assume complete markets. Complete market models, however, can not be used in all markets. To employ risk-neutral valuation and synthetic construction, as discussed above, one must study the markets carefully to see if the market satisfies the complete markets assumption.

3.5   Bubbles

An interesting economic phenomena that has been observed in financial markets are asset price bubbles. As asset price bubble exists when the market price of a risky asset exceeds its fundamental value.

Definition 3.11. A risky asset *price bubble* β_t is defined by

$$\beta_t = S_t - E^{\mathbb{Q}} \left(\frac{S_T}{B_T} | \mathcal{F}_t \right) B_t.$$

An asset price bubble exists in a market when ND is violated and there does not exist a risk-neutral probability $\mathbb{Q}$. In this case, at noted earlier, the risky asset will not be purchased and held for its final payoff without retrading. This can happen in both a complete and incomplete market.

Assuming only NFLVR, we get the following modification of the first fundamental theorem of asset pricing. This relaxation of the market structure allows the existence of asset price bubbles and gives an economic interpretation of a (strict) $\mathbb{Q}$ local martingale.

Theorem 3.12. *(First Fundamental Theorem of Asset Pricing)*
The market satisfies NFLVR if and only if there exists a probability $\mathbb{Q}$
equivalent to $\mathbb{P}$ *and a price bubble* $\beta_t \geq 0$ *such that*

$$S_t = E^{\mathbb{Q}} \left(\frac{S_T}{B_T} | \mathcal{F}_t \right) B_t + \beta_t \qquad \text{for all } t. \qquad (3.11)$$

For a proof see Jarrow and Protter [43].

This modification of the first fundamental theorem of asset pricing says that the market satisfies NFLVR if and only if there exists a probability $\mathbb{Q}$ equivalent to $\mathbb{P}$ such that the market price process equals its fundamental value plus a price bubble β_t. Hence, when $\frac{S_t}{B_t}$ is a $\mathbb{Q}$ (strict) local martingale, and *not* a $\mathbb{Q}$ martingale, there exists a strictly positive asset price bubble. This is the economic interpretation of a $\mathbb{Q}$ (strict) local martingale versus a $\mathbb{Q}$ martingale.

In expression (3.11), the asset price bubble is nonnegative, i.e. $\beta_t \geq 0$. It is nonnegative because the asset is always worth at least its value if purchased and held until liquidation (time T). The bubble represents the additional price paid for the asset above its fundamental value. This additional price paid is strictly positive if and only if one believes that after purchase, one can resell the asset for a higher price than its value if held forever.

We note that the bubble must vanish before or at time T, i.e. $\beta_T = 0$, because the expectation disappears at this date. It can be proven that if the bubble bursts before time T, it cannot be "reborn" (see Jarrow and Protter [43]).

The existence of an asset price bubble implies, in general, that the risk-neutral valuation formula does not work for pricing derivatives. It also implies that buying a risky asset is not the best way to obtain the asset's cash flows due to the possibility of the bubble bursting. Given ND is violated, one can obtain the same payoff more cheaply using an admissible self-financing trading strategy. Most models used in risk management impose assumptions that exclude bubbles, i.e. that imply ND. The user of risk management models must be aware of this limitation, especially if one believes that the relevant risky asset has a price bubble. In conclusion, we note that there is a methodology available for testing for the existence of asset pricing bubbles and pricing options in markets with bubbles. This is a new and exciting research area (see Jarrow and Protter [43] for a review).

Chapter 4

Market Risk (Interest Rates)

The BSM model assumes no interest rate risk. This is unrealistic and needs to be relaxed. Its relaxation is given by the Heath Jarrow Morton (HJM) model [23] extended to include risky assets as in Amin and Jarrow [1]. This is the content of this Chapter.

4.1   Set up

We start with the same basic structure as in the previous chapter. We consider a continuous time and finite horizon $[0, T]$ model. The uncertainty is captured by a filtered probability space satisfying the usual conditions $(\Omega, \mathcal{F}, (\mathcal{F}_t), \mathbb{P})$.

The extended HJM methodology is characterized by the following assumptions, many of which are identical to those introduced in the previous chapter.

Frictionless and competitive markets.

Frictionless means that there are no transactions costs and no trading constraints, e.g. short sale constraints or margin requirements. Competitive means that all traders act as price takers, believing that their trades have no quantity impact on the price.

Stochastic term structure of interest rates.

Traded are default-free zero-coupon bonds of all maturities with a time t price for the bond maturing at time τ denoted $P(t, \tau)$ for $0 \leq t \leq \tau \leq T$. Note that $P(t, t) = 1$ for all t. We assume that $P(t, \tau) > 0$ for all t, τ. The instantaneous forward rate at time t for maturity τ is implicitly defined by

$$P(t, \tau) = e^{-\int_t^\tau f(s, \tau) ds}. \tag{4.1}$$

Alternatively,

$$f(t, \tau) \triangle t \approx \frac{P(t, \tau)}{P(t, \tau + \triangle t)} - 1$$

for small $\triangle t$. This is the implicit borrowing rate embedded in the $P(t, \tau + \triangle t)$ zero-coupon bond at time t for the time period $[\tau, \tau + \triangle t]$.

We assume that given an initial forward rate curve $f(0, \tau) = f_0(\tau)$, the forward rate curve evolves as

$$f(t, \tau) = f_0(\tau) + \int_0^t \mu_f(s, \tau) ds + \sum_{k=1}^K \int_0^t \sigma_{f\,k}(s, \tau) dL_k(s) \tag{4.2}$$

where $(L_1(t), ..., L_K(t))$ are independent Brownian motions under $\mathbb{P}$ with $L_k(0) = 0$ all k. In this evolution the drift and volatilities $\mu_f(t, \tau), \sigma_{f\,k}(t, \tau)$ are very general stochastic processes, depending upon the state of the economy.

Over a small time interval $[t, t+\triangle t]$, this expression can be approximated by

$$\triangle f(t, \tau) = \mu_f(t, \tau) \triangle t + \sum_{k=1}^K \sigma_{f\,k}(t, \tau) \triangle L_k(t) \tag{4.3}$$

where $\triangle f(t, \tau) = f(t + \triangle t, \tau) - f(t, \tau)$ and $\triangle L_k(t) = L_k(t + \triangle t) - L_k(t)$.

Without loss of generality we assume that a money market account trades with initial value $B_0 = 1$ and time t value

$$B_t = e^{\int_0^t r(s) ds} \tag{4.4}$$

where $r(s) \equiv f(s, s)$ is the default-free spot rate of interest.

Risky asset price evolution.

Traded is a risky asset whose price at time t is denoted S_t. We assume that $S > 0$, that the risky asset has no cash flows, and that

$$S_t = S_0 + \int_0^t \mu_S(u) du + \sum_{k=0}^K \int_0^t \sigma_{S\,k}(u) dL_k(u) \tag{4.5}$$

where $L_0(t)$ is a Brownian motion with $L_0(0) = 0$ that is independent of the Brownian motions $(L_1(t), ..., L_K(t))$ and where $\mu_S, \sigma_{S\,k}$ for $k = 0, \ldots, K$ are very general stochastic processes, depending upon the state of the economy.

Over a small time interval $[t, t+\Delta t]$, this expression can be approximated by

$$\triangle S_t = \mu_S(t)\triangle t + \sum_{k=0}^{K} \sigma_{S\,k}(t)\triangle L_k(t).$$

The evolution for the term structure of interest rates has K factors generating the uncertainty $(L_1(t), ..., L_K(t))$, and the risky asset has these same K factors plus one more $L_0(t)$. The term structure model is said to follow a K- factor model. The K factors represent random shocks to the economy generated by fundamental macroeconomic activities, e.g. changes to the unemployment rate, inflation rate, monetary and fiscal policy. The factor $L_0(t)$ contains randomness unique to the risky asset and not shared by the interest rate process.

The trading strategies are as in Chapter 3, but expanded to include holding a finite number of the zero-coupon bonds $\tau_1, \ldots, \tau_K$ in addition to the money market account and risky asset, i.e. $(\alpha_B(t), \alpha_S(t), \alpha_1(t), \ldots, \alpha_K(t))$.

To guarantee the existence of a state price density, we assume that the drifts and volatilities of the term structure of interest rates and the risky asset price evolutions are restricted such that both NFLVR and ND hold. For the purposes of this chapter, we do not need to make these restrictions explicit. We note, however, that the restrictions on the forward rate evolution's drifts are known as the HJM arbitrage-free drift conditions (see Jarrow [29] for a review of the HJM model).

4.2   Results

Given this set up, we can now state the third fundamental theorem of asset pricing in the context of stochastic interest rates.

Theorem 4.1. *(The Third Fundamental Theorem)*
The market satisfies NFLVR and ND if and only if there exists a probability $\mathbb{Q}$ equivalent to $\mathbb{P}$ such that

$$
\begin{aligned}
S_t &= E^{\mathbb{Q}}\left(\tfrac{S_T}{B_T}\,|\mathcal{F}_t\right)B_t \qquad \text{for all } t, \quad \text{and} \\
P(t, \tau) &= E^{\mathbb{Q}}\left(\tfrac{1}{B_\tau}\,|\mathcal{F}_t\right)B_t \qquad \text{for all } t, \tau.
\end{aligned}
\tag{4.6}
$$

The proof is in Amin and Jarrow [1], extended by the insights from Jarrow and Larsson [38] to include ND.

As before, the probability $\mathbb{Q}$ is known as the risk-neutral probability.

For this theorem, the market need not be complete. As shown in the previous chapter, for pricing derivatives, we need a complete market. To ensure this, we add the following assumption (see Amin and Jarrow [1]).

(Completeness) For every $0 \leq \tau_1 \leq \ldots \leq \tau_K \leq T$, the volatility matrix

$$\begin{bmatrix} \sigma_{S0}(t) & \sigma_{S1}(t) & \sigma_{SK}(t) \\ 0 & \sigma_{f1}(t,\tau_1) & \sigma_{fK}(t,\tau_1) \\ \vdots & \vdots & \\ 0 & \sigma_{f1}(t,\tau_K) & \ldots & \sigma_{fK}(t,\tau_K) \end{bmatrix}$$

is non-singular for all t a.e. $\mathbb{P}$.

Extending the second fundamental theorem of asset pricing from Chapter 3 to this setting, as before, the market is complete if and only if the risk-neutral probability $\mathbb{Q}$ is unique.

4.3 Pricing

Just as before we can use risk-neutral valuation to price and hedge derivatives.

Let the payoff to a derivative $C_T \geq 0$ be nonnegative and $\mathcal{F}_T$−measurable. $\mathcal{F}_T$−measurable means that the payoff only depends on the information available at time T. This represents the set of all possible nonnegative random variables at time T, i.e. it is the set of all possible derivatives' payoffs; denote it $\mathcal{L}_+^0$.

Theorem 4.2. *(Risk-Neutral Valuation of Derivatives)*
Let the market satisfy NFLVR, ND, and be complete.
Let $\mathbb{Q}$ be the risk-neutral probability.
Then, given $C_T \in \mathcal{L}_+^0$ with $E^{\mathbb{Q}}\left(\frac{C_T}{B_T}\right) < \infty$,

$$C_t = E^{\mathbb{Q}}\left(\frac{C_T}{B_T}|\mathcal{F}_t\right) B_t \qquad \text{for all } t. \tag{4.7}$$

This theorem enables us to price interest rate derivatives and derivatives on the risky asset in a stochastic interest rate environment.

In a complete market, if any derivative does not satisfy this expression, then there is a trading opportunity - either an FLVR or a dominated security. This illustrates the first use of a no-arbitrage pricing model - pricing.

4.4 Synthetic Construction

When the market is complete, given a derivative $C_T \in \mathcal{L}_+^0$ with $E^{\mathbb{Q}}\left(\frac{C_T}{B_T}\right) < \infty$ where $\mathbb{Q}$ is the risk-neutral probability, there exists an admissible self-financing trading strategy

$$(\alpha_B(t), \alpha_S(t), \alpha_1(t), \ldots, \alpha_K(t))$$

in the money market account, risky asset, and zero-coupon bonds $\tau_1, \ldots, \tau_K$ that generates the derivative's payoffs, i.e. $C_T = X_T$. Letting the time t value of this trading strategy be denoted X_t we have that:

$$C_t = X_t = \alpha_B(t)B_t + \alpha_S(t)S_t + \sum_{k=1}^{K} \alpha_k(t)P(t, \tau_k). \qquad (4.8)$$

This implies that to synthetically construct the derivative's change in value over $[t, t+\triangle t]$, the number of units of the money market account must be $\alpha_B(t)$, the number of shares of the risky asset must be $\alpha_S(t)$, and the number of shares of the τ_k zero-coupon bond must be $\alpha_k(t)$ for $k = 1, \ldots, K$. The number of shares in the assets used to replicate the derivative's change in value are called the *hedge ratios*. This synthetic construction is the basis of the local risk management methods discussed in Part V below. This is the second use of a no-arbitrage model - hedging and risk management.

4.5 Bubbles

As in Chapter 3, an asset price bubble exists in this market when ND is violated and there does not exist a risk-neutral probability $\mathbb{Q}$ for the risky asset. Interestingly, if the default-free spot rate of interest is bounded below by a negative constant, i.e. $r_t \geq -c$ for $c \geq 0$, then a zero-coupon bond's price is bounded above, and the zero-coupon bonds can have no price bubbles (see Jarrow and Protter [43]). In this case, $\mathbb{Q}$ is a risk-neutral measure for the zero-coupon bonds, even though it may not be for the risky asset. We point out that in recent times, the default-free spot rate of many countries have be negative.

Assuming only NFLVR, we summarize this observation with the following modification of the first fundamental theorem of asset pricing in the context of stochastic interest rates.

Theorem 4.3. *(First Fundamental Theorem of Asset Pricing)*

Assume $r_t \geq -c$ for $c \geq 0$. The market satisfies NFLVR if and only if there exists a probability $\mathbb{Q}$ equivalent to $\mathbb{P}$ and a price bubble $\beta_t \geq 0$ such that

$$S_t = E^{\mathbb{Q}} \left(\frac{S_T}{B_T} \mid \mathcal{F}_t \right) B_t + \beta_t \qquad \text{for all } t, \quad \text{and}$$

$$P(t, \tau) = E^{\mathbb{Q}} \left(\frac{1}{B_\tau} \mid \mathcal{F}_t \right) B_t \qquad \text{for all } t, \tau. \tag{4.9}$$

The existence of an asset price bubble implies, in general, that the risk-neutral valuation formula does not work for pricing derivatives on the risky asset. It also implies that buying a risky asset may not be best way to obtain the asset's cash flows due to the possibility of the bubble bursting. Given ND is violated, one can obtain the same payoff more cheaply using a self-financing trading strategy. Here, however, risk-neutral valuation still works for pricing interest rate derivatives. Most models used in risk management impose assumptions that exclude bubbles, i.e. imply ND. The user of risk management models must be aware of this limitation for pricing derivatives on the risky asset if she believes the risky asset is exhibiting a bubble.

Chapter 5

Credit Risk

This chapter studies the reduced form models for pricing and hedging credit risk created by Jarrow and Turnbull [44, 45]. Credit risk exists whenever two counter parties engage in borrowing and lending. Borrowing can be in cash, which is the standard case, or it can be through the 'shorting' of securities. *Shorting* a security is selling a security one does not own. To do this, the security must first be borrowed from an intermediate counterparty, with an obligation to return the borrowed security at a later date. The borrowing part of this shorting transaction involves credit risk. Since the majority of transactions in financial and commodity markets involve some sort of borrowing, understanding the economics of credit risk is fundamental to the broader understanding of economics itself.

5.1 Set up

We start with the same basic structure as in the previous chapter, except that we replace the traded risky asset with a risky zero-coupon bond. We consider a continuous time and finite horizon $[0, T]$ model. The uncertainty is captured by a filtered probability space satisfying the usual conditions $(\Omega, \mathcal{F}, (\mathcal{F}_t), \mathbb{P})$.

The reduced form model is characterized by the following assumptions, many of which are identical to those given in the previous chapters.

Frictionless and competitive markets.

Frictionless means that there are no transactions costs and no trading constraints, e.g. short sale constraints or margin requirements. Competitive means that all traders act as price takers, believing that their trades have no quantity impact on the price.

Stochastic term structure of interest rates.

Traded are default-free zero-coupon bonds of all maturities with a time t price for the bond maturing at time τ denoted $P(t, \tau)$ for $0 \leq t \leq \tau \leq T$. Note that $P(t, t) = 1$ for all t. We assume that $P(t, \tau) > 0$ for all t, τ. The instantaneous forward rate at time t for maturity τ is implicitly defined by

$$P(t, \tau) = e^{-\int_t^\tau f(s,\tau)ds}. \tag{5.1}$$

We assume that given an initial forward rate curve $f(0, \tau) = f_0(\tau)$, the forward rate curve evolves as

$$f(t, \tau) = f_0(\tau) + \int_0^t \mu_f(s, \tau)ds + \sum_{k=1}^K \int_0^t \sigma_{f\,k}(s, \tau)dL_k(s) \tag{5.2}$$

where $(L_1(t), ..., L_K(t))$ are independent Brownian motions under $\mathbb{P}$ with $L_k(0) = 0$ for $k = 1, \ldots, K$, and where the drift and volatilities $\mu_f(t, \tau), \sigma_{f\,k}$ (t, τ) for $k = 1, \ldots, K$ are very general stochastic processes, depending upon the state of the economy.

Without loss of generality we assume that a money market account trades with initial value $B_0 = 1$ and time t value

$$B_t = e^{\int_0^t r(s)ds} \tag{5.3}$$

where $r(s) \equiv f(s, s)$ is the default-free spot rate of interest.

Risky zero-coupon bond default process.

Traded is a risky zero-coupon bond issued by a credit entity *promising* to pay a dollar at time $\tau \leq T$ with time $t \in [0, T]$ price denoted $D(t, \tau)$. The promise may not be kept, which is why the zero-coupon bond is risky. To derive the evolution of the risky zero-coupon bond, we need to understand its payoffs. In this regard, we need to understand when the entity defaults and the recovery rate on the zero-coupon bond in the event of default. For simplicity of terminology, let's call this credit entity a firm.

The firm can have many outstanding liabilities, but one of them is this zero-coupon bond. These liabilities have contractual payments to be made by the firm at various times over the lives of the contracts. The first time the firm does not make a contractual payment on any of its liabilities, the firm is in "default" on that liability's payments. Due to cross-defaulting provisions, this means that all of the firm's liabilities are in default too (usually all contractual payments - interest owed and principal outstanding - become due). We want to characterize this default process and the recovery rate on the zero-coupon bond if default occurs.

Let $Z_t = (Z_1(t), \ldots, Z_m(t))$ be a collection of stochastic processes characterizing the state of the economy at time t. These stochastic processes include macroeconomic variables, e.g. the inflation rate, unemployment rate, etc. A subset of these could be a finite number of the default-free forward rates or market indices.

Let $\chi \in [0, T]$ be a stopping time with respect to the filtration $\mathcal{F}_t$ denoting the firm's default time. This default time generates a point process

$$1_{\chi \geq t} = \begin{cases} 1 & \text{if} & \chi \geq t \\ 0 & \text{otherwise} \end{cases} .$$

We assume that the point process $1_{\chi \geq t}$ is a Cox process with intensity $\lambda_t \equiv \lambda_t(Z_t) \geq 0$. This means that conditional upon the vector of state processes Z_t for all $t \in [0, T]$, it behaves like a Poisson process (see Jarrow [30] for a proof of these statements). The default intensity λ_t is the probability of the firm defaulting over a small time interval $[t, t + \Delta]$ conditional on no default prior to time t.

If the firm defaults prior to the zero-coupon bond's maturity date τ, we assume that the bond receives a *recovery payment* less than or equal to the promised dollar at time τ, i.e.

$$D(\tau, \tau) = \begin{cases} \frac{R(\chi, \tau) B(\tau)}{B(\chi)} \leq 1 & \text{if } \chi \leq \tau \\ 1 & \text{if } \chi > \tau \end{cases} \tag{5.4}$$

where $1 \geq R(\chi, \tau) \geq 0$. Three recovery rate processes are frequently used in the literature.

Recovery of Face Value.

$$R(\chi, \tau) \equiv \delta \text{ where } \delta \in [0, 1].$$

Recovery of Treasury.

$$R(\chi, \tau) \equiv \delta P(\chi, \tau) \text{ where } \delta \in [0, 1].$$

This states that on the default date, the debt is worth some constant percentage of an otherwise equivalent, but default-free zero-coupon bond.

Recovery of Market Value.

$$R(\chi, \mathcal{T}) \equiv \delta D(\chi-, \tau) \text{ where } \delta \in [0, 1]$$

and $D(\chi-, \tau) \equiv \lim_{t \to \chi, t \leq \chi} D(t, \tau)$ is the value of the debt issue an instant before default. This states that on the default date, the debt is worth some constant fraction of its value an instant before default, at time $\chi-$.

In summary, the evolution for the term structure of interest rates has K factors generating the uncertainty, and the zero-coupon bond's payoffs are generated by a default process with intensity $\lambda(Z_t)$ and recovery rate $R(\chi, \tau)$.

The trading strategies are as in Chapter 4, but replacing the risky asset with the risky zero-coupon bond, hence, a trading strategy includes holding a finite number of the zero-coupon bonds $\tau_1, \ldots, \tau_K$ in addition to the money market account and the risky zero-coupon bond, i.e. $(\alpha_B(t), \alpha_1(t), \ldots, \alpha_K(t), \alpha_D(t))$.

5.2 Results

To guarantee the existence of a state price density, we assume that NFLVR and ND hold.

Given this set up, we can now state the third fundamental theorem of asset pricing in the context of credit risk and stochastic interest rates.

Theorem 5.1. *(The Third Fundamental Theorem)*
The market satisfies NFLVR and ND if and only if there exists a probability $\mathbb{Q}$ equivalent to $\mathbb{P}$ such that

$$D(t, \tau) = E^{\mathbb{Q}} \left(\frac{D(\tau, \tau)}{B_\tau} \,|\, \mathcal{F}_t \right) B_t \qquad \text{for all } t, \tau, \quad \text{and}$$

$$P(t, \tau) = E^{\mathbb{Q}} \left(\frac{1}{B_\tau} \,|\, \mathcal{F}_t \right) B_t \qquad \text{for all } t, \tau. \tag{5.5}$$

Proof. The theorem from Chapter 4 applies with the risky zero-coupon bond instead of the risky asset.

As before, the probability $\mathbb{Q}$ is known as the risk-neutral probability. We point out that the equation for $D(t, \tau)$ in this theorem completely characterizes the stochastic evolution of the risky zero-coupon bond's price as a function of default-free interest rates, the information filtration, the risky zero-coupon bond's default process, and the risk-neutral probability $\mathbb{Q}$.

5.3 Pricing

Just as before we can use risk-neutral valuation to price and hedge derivatives if the market is complete. By the second fundamental theorem of asset pricing, extended to this economy, the market is complete if and only if the risk-neutral probability is unique.

Let $C_T \geq 0$ be nonnegative and $\mathcal{F}_T$−measurable. This represents the set of all possible nonnegative random variables at time T, i.e. it is the set of all possible derivatives' payoffs; denote it $\mathcal{L}_+^0$.

Theorem 5.2. *Risk-Neutral Valuation of Derivatives*
   Let the market satisfy NFLVR, ND, and be complete.
   Let $\mathbb{Q}$ be the risk-neutral probability.
   Then, given $C_T \in \mathcal{L}_+^0$ with $E^{\mathbb{Q}}\left(\frac{C_T}{B_T}\right) < \infty$,

$$C_t = E^{\mathbb{Q}}\left(\frac{C_T}{B_T} \,|\, \mathcal{F}_t\right) B_t \qquad for\ all\ t. \tag{5.6}$$

    This theorem enables us to price interest rate and credit derivatives. In a complete market, if any derivative does not satisfy this expression, then there is a trading opportunity - either a FLVR or a dominated security. In either case, trading profits are available. This is one use of the no-arbitrage pricing model - pricing.

    If the market is incomplete, then the risk-neutral probability is not unique. In fact, there are an infinite number of such probabilities satisfying the first fundamental theorem. To price credit derivatives, we need to select a unique risk-neutral probability $\mathbb{Q}$ from the set of possible risk-neutral probabilities. We do this by assuming that sufficient credit derivatives trade such that the extended market is complete. Then, by the second fundamental theorem of asset pricing, their market prices uniquely determine the risk-neutral probability $\mathbb{Q}$. We say that this unique risk-neutral probability is "chosen by the market." Pricing is then given by expression (5.6) using the risk-neutral probability chosen by the market in this expanded market.

5.4   Synthetic Construction

If the market is complete, given a derivative $C_T \in \mathcal{L}_+^0$ with $E^{\mathbb{Q}}\left(\frac{C_T}{B_T}\right) < \infty$ where $\mathbb{Q}$ is the risk-neutral probability, there exists an admissible self-financing trading strategy
$$(\alpha_B(t), \alpha_1(t), \ldots, \alpha_K(t), \alpha_D(t))$$
in the money market account, the default-free zero-coupon bonds $\tau_1, \ldots, \tau_K$, and the risky zero-coupon bond that generates the derivative's payoffs, i.e. $C_T = X_T$. Letting the time t value of this trading strategy be denoted X_t we have that:

$$C_t = X_t = \alpha_B(t)B_t + \sum_{k=1}^{K} \alpha_k(t)P(t, \tau_k) + \alpha_D(t)D(t, \tau). \tag{5.7}$$

This implies that to synthetically construct the derivative security's change in value over $[t, t + \triangle t]$, the number of units of the money market account must be $\alpha_B(t)$, the number of shares of the τ_k zero-coupon bond must be $\alpha_k(t)$ for $k = 1, \ldots, K$, and the number of shares of the risky zero-coupon bond must be $\alpha_D(t)$. The number of shares in the assets used to replicate the derivative's change in value are called the *hedge ratios*. This synthetic construction is the basis of the local risk management methods discussed in Part V below. This is the second use of a no-arbitrage model - hedging and risk management.

When considering credit risk, the markets are normally incomplete. This is because when modeling default as generated by a Cox process with a jump in the bond price at default (due to random recovery rates), the resulting risky debt price process will imply an incomplete market. In this case, exact synthetic construction of a credit derivative is not possible. Consequently, risk managing a portfolio of risky bonds involves the use of traded risky bonds and credit derivatives, and not self-financing trading strategies of risky zero-coupon bonds. This is called static hedging as opposed to dynamic hedging. We will discuss both dynamic and static hedging later in the book.

5.5   Bubbles

When ND is violated, price bubbles become a possibility. However, when considering bonds, bubbles usually do not exist. If the default-free spot rate of interest is bounded below, i.e. $r_t \geq -c$ for $c \geq 0$, then both the default-free and risky zero-coupon bonds' prices are bounded above. In this case none of the zero-coupon bonds can have price bubbles (see Jarrow and Protter [43] for a proof). Consequently, in this case assuming only NFLVR we get the following modification of the first fundamental theorem of asset pricing in the context of credit risk and stochastic interest rates.

Theorem 5.3. *(First Fundamental Theorem of Asset Pricing)*
Assume $r_t \geq -c$ for $c \geq 0$. The market satisfies NFLVR if and only if there exists a probability $\mathbb{Q}$ equivalent to $\mathbb{P}$ such that

$$D(t,\tau) = E^{\mathbb{Q}}\left(\frac{D(\tau,\tau)}{B_\tau}\,|\mathcal{F}_t\right) B_t \qquad \text{for all } t, \tau, \quad \text{and}$$
$$P(t,\tau) = E^{\mathbb{Q}}\left(\frac{1}{B_\tau}\,|\mathcal{F}_t\right) B_t \qquad \text{for all } t, \tau. \tag{5.8}$$

This theorem, along with risk-neutral valuation, is the basis for pricing and hedging credit risky assets. As shown, bubbles play no role in these markets because with interest rates that are bounded below and cannot become too negative, they do not exist.

Chapter 6

Liquidity Risk

Liquidity risk occurs when we relax the competitive market assumption and there is a quantity impact on the price from trading an asset, i.e. the more units of an asset one buys, the larger the purchase price per share paid, and the more units of an asset one sells, the smaller the selling price per share received. There are two cases to be studied: a temporary and a permanent quantity impact on the price. A temporary impact on the price occurs when the quantity impact only lasts for an instant, and disappears after the trade is executed. When temporary, the quantity impact on the price is analogous to a transaction cost. As such, the trade has no effect on the future evolution of the asset price process. A permanent impact on the price occurs when the quantity impact lasts for a finite time interval and affects the future evolution of the asset price process. This chapter discusses both of these possibilities.

6.1 Temporary Quantity Impact on the Price

This section studies liquidity risk when there is a temporary quantity impact on the price from trading that lasts only an instant. As such, the trade has no effect on the asset price's future evolution. This section follows Cetin, Jarrow, Protter [10] and Cetin, Soner, Touzi [11]. It will be shown that a temporary quantity impact from trading on the price affects valuation and hedging analogous to the manner in which transaction costs affect these results: markets are incomplete and exact synthetic construction and unique pricing of derivatives fails. In fact, transaction costs can be viewed as a special case of the subsequent analysis.

6.1.1   Set up

For the purposes of this chapter we use a modification of the set up in Chapter 3. We consider a continuous time and finite horizon $[0, T]$ model. The uncertainty is captured by a filtered probability space satisfying the usual conditions $(\Omega, \mathcal{F}, (\mathcal{F}_t), \mathbb{P})$.

We relax the competitive and frictionless market assumptions. Instead, we impose the following assumptions.

No trading constraints.

There are no trading constraints, e.g. short sale constraints or margin requirements.

Note that this analysis allows there to be transaction costs from trading.

Interest rate risk.

Traded is a money market account with initial value $B_0 = 1$ and time t value

$$B_t = e^{\int_0^t r(s)ds} \tag{6.1}$$

where $r(s)$ is the default-free spot rate of interest. This is a stochastic process which is $\mathcal{F}_s$ - measurable.

Risky asset price evolution.

Traded is a risky asset with no cash flows. To incorporate liquidity costs from trading, we assume that there is a *supply curve* for trading the risky asset. This supply curve gives the price paid/received of the risky asset, per share, at time t for transacting v shares. Different prices are paid/received for different quantities traded. Hence, there is a quantity impact from trading on the price of the risky asset.

To construct this supply curve, we begin by considering the time t *marginal price*, defined as the time t market price for zero shares traded, denoted S_t. This is a conceptualization, it represents the limit of the price as the quantity of shares transacted approaches zero. Alternatively, one can think of this as the "true" price in a competitive and frictionless world.

We assume that the marginal price $S_t > 0$ and that it evolves as

$$S_t = S_0 + \int_0^t \mu_S(u)du + \int_0^t \sigma_S(u)dL(u)$$

where $L(t)$ is a Brownian motion under $\mathbb{P}$ with $L(0) = 0$, the drift μ_S is a very general stochastic process depending upon the state of the economy that satisfies the necessary measurability and integrability conditions so that the relevant integral is well defined, and the volatility σ_S is a stochastic process that is bounded and Lipschitz continuous.

Over a small time interval $[t, t+\Delta t]$, this expression can be approximated by

$$\triangle S_t = \mu_S(t)\triangle t + \sigma_S(t)\triangle L(t) \tag{6.2}$$

where $\triangle S_t = S_{t+\triangle t} - S_t$ and $\triangle L(t) = L(t + \triangle t) - L(t)$.

Given this marginal price, we assume that the price paid/received of the risky asset, per share, at time t for transacting v shares is

$$\mathbb{S}(t, S_t(\omega), v)$$

where (i) given S_t, $\mathbb{S}(t, \cdot, v)$ is a deterministic function of t, v, and (ii) it is continuously differentiable and increasing in v, i.e.

$$\frac{\partial \mathbb{S}(t, S_t, v)}{\partial v} > 0.$$

The increasing assumption means that as the shares purchased increase, the price per share increases. Conversely, as the shares sold increase, the price per share received declines. This is the normal situation in financial markets, reflecting both asymmetric information across traders and portfolio rebalancing adjustment costs.

Last, to simplify the analysis we assume that the supply curve is horizontal at time T, i.e. there are no liquidity costs at time T.

Assumption. *(No Time T Quantity Impact on the Price)*

$$\mathbb{S}(T, S_T, v) = S_T \ for \ all \ v.$$

The assumption of no cash flows on the risky asset is for simplicity of the presentation and can easily be relaxed. We consider only one risky asset, but this is also easily extended to many traded risky assets.

Given these assumptions, we now need to discuss how liquidity considerations change trading strategies.

Definition 6.1. A *trading strategy* with initial wealth x is defined to be a specification of the holdings in the money market account and risky asset, $(\alpha_B(t), \alpha_S(t))$ for all t that is predictable with respect to $(\mathcal{F}_t)$. Predictable means that the trading strategy can only depend on information from the past and the present (in a left-continuous manner), see Protter [56]. We assume that this trading strategy is continuous in time with at most a finite (but random) number of discrete jumps over $[0, T]$ corresponding to large purchases or sales at any instant.

We note immediately that given a supply curve, there is no unique value for a portfolio unless a trading strategy is first specified. Indeed, the share holdings in the risky asset can be valued at any point along the supply curve yielding a different value. Two values immediately can be identified. The first is the *liquidation value*. This is the value of the portfolio obtained by valuing the shares at their immediate liquidation value, i.e. $\mathbb{S}(t, S_t, \alpha_S(t-))$. The second is the *marked-to-market value* obtained by valuing the risky asset shares at the marginal price S_t. The implicit assumption here is that no trades are executed. The marked-to-market value will play a significant role in the subsequent analysis.

Definition 6.2. The time t *marked-to-market value* of the trading strategy $(\alpha_B(t), \alpha_S(t))$ is

$$X_t^{\alpha_B, \alpha_S} = \alpha_B(t)B_t + \alpha_S(t)S_t \tag{6.3}$$

where $X_0^{\alpha_B, \alpha_S} = x$.

When buying and selling the risky asset across time, liquidity costs reduce the marked-to-market value of the portfolio. Extending the notion of a self-financing trading strategy needs to incorporate these liquidity costs. The following definition applies.

Definition 6.3. Consider the trading strategy $(\alpha_B(t), \alpha_S(t))$. Let $\tau_1, ..., \tau_N$ be the times when discrete trades take place in this trading strategy over the time interval $[0, t)$. At all other times the trading strategy is continuous.

The trading strategy with marked-to-market value process $X_t^{\alpha_B, \alpha_S}$ is said to be *self-financing* if

$$X_t^{\alpha_B, \alpha_S} = x + \int_0^t (\alpha_B(u)dB_u + \alpha_S(u)dS_u) - \int_0^t \left(\frac{\partial \mathbb{S}(u, S_u, 0)}{\partial v} \right) d[\alpha_S, \alpha_S]_u^c$$
$$- \sum_{k=1}^N \triangle \alpha_S(\tau_k) \left(\mathbb{S}(\tau_k, S_{\tau_k}, \triangle \alpha_S(\tau_k)) - S_{\tau_k} \right) \tag{6.4}$$

where $[\alpha_S, \alpha_S]_t^c$ is the continuous part of the quadratic variation (for a definition of the quadratic variation, see Protter [56]).

In this definition, the liquidity costs from trading are represented by the last two terms, both of which enter negatively. The first is the liquidity costs generated by continuous trading while the second is the liquidity costs generated by discrete trading. The discrete trading liquidity costs are intuitive as $(\mathbb{S}(\tau_k, S_{\tau_k}, \triangle \alpha_S(\tau_k)) - S_{\tau_k})$ represents the quantity impact on the price from trading $\triangle \alpha_S(\tau_k)$ shares at time τ_k. Both of these costs reduce the marked-to-market value of the portfolio.

Remark. (High Frequency Traders (HF))

Under the above structure, doubling strategies are possible, and they need to be excluded. To do this we could add a uniform credit constraint, a lower bound on the marked-to-market value of the trading strategy as in Chapter 3.

With this uniform lower bound, it can be shown that a trader can avoid all liquidity costs by trading continuously with finite variation trading strategies (see Cetin, Jarrow, Protter [10]). These trading strategies can be interpreted as those employed by HF traders. Ordinary traders cannot use these liquidity cost avoiding trading strategies because of the speed of trading implied.

These liquidity cost avoiding trading strategies also enable the HF traders to approximate any derivative's payoffs as closely as desired (in an L^2 sense). This also implies that for an HF trader, the standard pricing and hedging results for derivatives apply as in Chapter 3, but using these liquidity cost avoiding trading strategies.

In practice, these liquidity cost avoiding trading strategies have the characteristic that they are not scalable, i.e. $(\alpha_B(t), \alpha_S(t))$ are uniformly bounded in absolute value. This boundedness restriction implies that the HF traders can generate limited arbitrage opportunities by trading derivatives against ordinary traders. The arbitrage profits are limited precisely because the trading strategies are bounded in absolute value. As such, in equilibrium, the market prices of derivatives will still reflect the trading activities of ordinary traders who cannot use these liquidity cost avoiding trading strategies. The subsequent analysis focuses on these ordinary traders. This completes the remark.

To exclude both doubling strategies and liquidity cost avoiding trading strategies we need to add some additional restrictions on the trading strategies that can be employed. We now introduce these additional restrictions.

Definition 6.4. A self-financing trading strategy $(\alpha_B(t), \alpha_S(t))$ with marked-to-market value process $X_t^{\alpha_B, \alpha_S}$ is said to be *admissible* if the position in the money market account is restricted in the following way.

Let $\tau_1, ..., \tau_N$ be the times when discrete trades take place over the time interval $[0, t)$. There must exist processes η_u, Γ_u satisfying various measurability and integrability conditions (see Cetin, Soner, Touzi [11], p. 324) and $\mathcal{F}(\tau_k)$ - measurable random variables $y(\tau_k)$ such that the shares in the risky asset $(\alpha_S(t))$ are of the form

$$\alpha_S(t) = \sum_{k=1}^N y(\tau_k) 1_{T > t \geq \tau_k} + \int_0^t \left(\eta_u du + \Gamma_u d\left(\frac{S_u}{B_u} \right) \right).$$

Let $\mathcal{A}(x)$ be the set of all admissible self-financing trading strategies starting with initial wealth x.

6.1.2   Results

We can now state our first result, which is related to the third fundamental theorem of asset pricing.

Theorem 6.5. *(Sufficient Condition for NFLVR)*
   Assume there exists a probability $\mathbb{Q}$ *equivalent to* $\mathbb{P}$ *such that*

$$S_t = E^{\mathbb{Q}} \left(\frac{S_T}{B_T} \,|\mathcal{F}_t \right) B_t \qquad for\ all\ t. \tag{6.5}$$

Then, NFLVR is true.

For a proof use Cetin, Jarrow, Protter [10] as applied to Cetin, Soner, Touzi [11].

The idea underlying the proof of this theorem is that if there are no arbitrage opportunities without liquidity costs, which is what the existence of a risk-neutral probability implies, then no more can be introduced by making trading more costly. In the definition of NFLVR, the liquidity costs of trading are included in the trading strategies allowed in the set $\mathcal{A}(x)$ as defined above. Note that this theorem is not an if and only if proposition. For applications, this theorem is sufficient because one normally starts the application by assuming that the evolution satisfies expression (6.5), which implies the market satisfies NFLVR. This no-arbitrage condition is what is needed for pricing and hedging.

6.1.3   Pricing and Synthetic Construction

This section discusses the pricing and hedging of derivatives. For the purposes of liquidity risk, we define a derivative as any function of B_T, S_T, denoted $g(B_T, S_T)$, which is Borel measurable, bounded from below, and satisfies an affine growth condition (see Cetin, Soner, Touzi [11], p. 325). Although technical in nature, these are only mild restrictions on the set of derivatives. They are included in order to make the following definitions meaningful.

Due to liquidity costs, it is easy to see from expression (6.4) that markets will no longer be complete. This is because liquidity costs reduce the value of the portfolio, so that at time T liquidation, significant value will be lost when trying to create derivatives whose payoffs are non-linear functions of B_T, S_T. If the payoffs are non-linear, static trades will not replicate the payoffs to the derivative and dynamic trading is required. This fact implies that we can no longer synthetically construct any derivative's payoff. Hence, there will not be a unique arbitrage-free price for a derivative.

However, we can define upper and lower prices for a derivative. If the derivative's price ever exceeds these bounds, then an arbitrage opportunity exists. The upper price is defined as follows.

Definition 6.6. Given a derivative C_T, the *super-replication price* is defined by

$$\overline{C}_t = inf\left\{x : \exists(\alpha_B(t), \alpha_S(t)) \in \mathcal{A}(x) \ s.t. \ X_T^{\alpha_B, \alpha_S} \geq C_T\right\}. \tag{6.6}$$

The super-replication price corresponds to the smallest amount x one can invest to sell the derivative and pay off the derivative's liabilities with the proceeds from the investment. The lower price is defined analogously.

Definition 6.7. Given a derivative C_T, the *sub-replication price* is defined by

$$\underline{C}_t = sup\left\{x : \exists(\alpha_B(t), \alpha_S(t)) \in \mathcal{A}(x) \ s.t. \ X_T^{\alpha_B, \alpha_S} \leq C_T\right\}. \tag{6.7}$$

The sub-replication price corresponds to the largest amount x one can borrow to buy the derivative and pay off the loan with the proceeds from the derivative.

Given these concepts, we get the following result.

Theorem 6.8. *(Super- and Sub-Replication Prices)*
Assume there exists a probability $\mathbb{Q}$ equivalent to $\mathbb{P}$ such that expression (6.5) holds.
Given a derivative C_T with $E^\mathbb{Q}\left(\frac{C_T}{B_T}\right) < \infty$, then

$$\overline{C}_t \geq E^\mathbb{Q}\left(\frac{C_T}{B_T} | \mathcal{F}_t\right) B_t \geq \underline{C}_t \tag{6.8}$$

for all t.
The inequality is strict for a derivative C_T that is a non-linear function of B_T, S_T.

For a proof see Cetin, Soner, Touzi [11], Corollary 3.4.

To get exact values for $\overline{C}_t, \underline{C}_t$, one needs to solve the optimization problems given in the definitions of the super- and sub-replication prices. This is a difficult exercise that almost always requires a numerical procedure. Similarly, the super- and sub- replication strategies must be obtained numerically as well. Thus, these procedures are not often employed. In practice, due to the complexity of these computations, either liquidity costs are ignored (they are often small for financial institutions) or static hedging of derivatives using other traded assets and derivatives is used instead. Static hedging is studied later in the book.

6.2   Permanent Quantity Impact on the Price

This section studies the pricing and hedging of derivatives when trades have a permanent quantity impact on the price. This section is based on Jarrow [25, 26]. Permanent quantity impacts from trading on the price normally apply to only "large traders," financial institutions, when trading in large quantities.

6.2.1   Market Manipulation

When trades have a permanent quantity impact on the price, the asset price's future evolution changes and depends on the investor's trading strategy. As such, *market manipulation*, the creation of arbitrage or profitable trading strategies earning excess returns due to strategic trading become possible.

To illustrate some of the issues involved, we discuss two examples of market manipulation.

Example. *(Market Corner and Short Squeeze)*
A *market corner and short squeeze* happens as follows. Let the total number of outstanding shares of the risky asset be N. Suppose that individual Sh shorts the risky asset. This implies there are more shares outstanding than the initial supply equalling N + shorted shares.

Now, suppose that individual Lo buys all the outstanding shares plus the shorted shares. Since individual Lo owns all the available shares, he is the one who has lent them to the short seller. They are deliverable upon demand of the stock lender.

Next, individual Lo demands the borrowed shares to be returned. Individual Sh has no choice but to buy them back from individual Lo. Since individual Lo owns all the shares, he can demand any price he wishes. This is a market corner and short squeeze. We note that this strategy is an arbitrage opportunity because it generates riskless profits. In most markets, this is an illegal trading activity.

Example. *(Pump and Dump Trading Strategy)*

A *pump and dump trading strategy* happens as follows. Suppose there is a permanent quantity impact on the price when a large trader buys large quantities over a short period of time, but not when the large trader sells smaller quantities over a longer time period. The trading strategy is to buy large quantities, continually, driving the price up. Then, when the price is high enough, to slowly sell the purchased shares. Given the differential permanence of the quantity impact on the price when the price is going up versus when it is going down, this generates riskless profits. This trading strategy also creates a price bubble, where the fundamental value is defined to be the market price without including the impact of the large trader.

6.2.2 Pricing and Hedging Derivatives

In this setting, the BSM methodologies for pricing and hedging derivatives no longer apply. This follows because the price process is no longer completely exogenous, but depends both on the "fundamental value" (exogenous) and the trading strategies of investors in the market. Because these trading strategies can change over time, there is no reason to believe that patterns in historical price series reflect the future evolution of the asset's price process. Trading, valuation, and hedging become a complex strategic and noncooperative game.

To show why the standard pricing and hedging methodologies fail we give a simple example.

Example. *(Expiring near-the-money call)*

This example assumes familiarity with the Black-Scholes (BS) European call option formula, see Jarrow and Chatterjea [37]. Let's consider a European call option on the risky asset with strike price K and maturity date T. Suppose we are at time $T - \varepsilon$ for $\varepsilon > 0$ a small number. Let the risky asset price be $S_{T-\varepsilon} = K - \delta$ for $\delta > 0$ a small number. The stock in almost at expiration and near-the-money. Finally, suppose that in the absence of a large trader, the risky asset price process follows geometric Brownian motion with a volatility of $\sigma > 0$.

If one uses the BS call option formula, the value of the call option is $C_{T-\varepsilon} \approx 0$, because the call is out-of-the money, there is not much time left until maturity, and the volatility is bounded. The option's delta is $N \approx 0$ since the option is going to expire out-of-the-money with probability near one.

Now, consider a large trader who knows there is a permanent quantity impact on the price from trading. She first buys the call options in large quantities, getting her position for nearly 0 dollars. Next, she buys the risky asset in large quantities, driving the price up at maturity to be much larger than the strike price, i.e. $S_T \gg K$. The option expires in-the-money. After the options expire, she liquidates her stock position slowly to minimize the liquidity costs.

This trader makes riskless arbitrage profits. This occurs because the gains on the option position being highly leveraged dominate the liquidation costs of buying and selling the underlying stock.

Note that the true price of the option, given the large trader's strategy, is $C_{T-\varepsilon} \approx S_T - K \gg 0$ and the true delta is $N \approx 1$. The BSM pricing and hedging methodology could not have been more incorrect.

6.2.3   Conclusion

For risk management purposes, whether strategic trading and market manipulation are relevant depends on the specific market and the market conditions present at any point in time. It depends on whether trading by large traders have a permanent quantity impact on the price or not. In high volume actively traded markets, permanent quantity impacts on the price from trading are most likely rare. In small volume and inactively traded markets, permanent quantity impacts are more likely. Understanding the market and monitoring who is trading in the market and why will facilitate recognizing when such large trader liquidity risk arises.

If permanent quantity impacts from trading on the price are not likely, the no-arbitrage pricing and hedging methodology provides a good first approximation. When permanent quantity impacts from trading on the price are possible, the no-arbitrage pricing and hedging methodology does not apply. Risk management decision making in these noncompetitive market environments is not well understood.

It is important to note that the no-arbitrage pricing and hedging methodology is regularly and successfully used in practice by financial institutions in many markets. Consequently, this observation suggests that the situations where the methodology fails to apply are rare, especially for high volume actively traded markets. Nonetheless, just because their use is prevalent, doesn't mean that their usage cannot be improved. Proper usage requires a careful monitoring of financial markets for large trader liquidity risk situations, and when observed not basing risk management decisions on the no-arbitrage methodologies.

Chapter 7

Operational Risk

This chapter briefly discusses operational risk.

7.1 Management and Accounting Controls

By definition, operational risk is the risk that losses will occur when an individual manages a portfolio or a firm manages a balance sheet due to mismanagement, fraud, legal errors, and execution errors in the purchase/sale of assets. If one considers the execution of a trade as a production process, then anything that goes wrong in the production process is operational risk. As such, controlling operational risk within the firm is a managerial problem.

Operational risk can be controlled by good management and accounting procedures. There have been many cases (see Part VI) where operational risk has caused a financial institution to lose billions of dollars and even fail. The realm of proper internal management and accounting procedures, although very important, is outside the scope of this book.

7.2 Risk Management

When the market values a firm's equity, it implicitly includes within this valuation the probability that an operational risk event within the firm will cause losses. As with any other event that can cause losses to a firm's balance sheet, operational risk events and losses can be modeled. This modeling is especially important for the internal risk management of banks because it is an input to the regulatory risk measures employed for the determination of their regulatory capital, see Part IV, Chapter 11.

Fortunately, the modeling of operational risk events is analogous to that used to model default when considering credit risk. As such, tools and procedures for this modeling are already well developed. To complete our discussion of modeling operational risk, therefore, it is sufficient to make explicit the analogy. The identification is as follows: (i) equate the default time to the time of an operational risk event, and (ii) equate the recovery rate in the event of default to "one minus the loss rate" in the event of an operational risk event. Given a stochastic process for the operational risk event time and recovery rate, this identification completely describes the loss process for an operational risk event.

Data bases are available for estimating the intensity process of an operational risk event and the losses given an operational risk event occurs. The statistical tools employed are the same as those used to estimate the default process, for additional details see Jarrow [28] and Jarrow, Oxman, Yildirim [39].

Chapter 8

Trading Constraints

This chapter discusses the impact of trading constraints on pricing and hedging in arbitrage-free markets. Trading constraints are important because in almost all of the risk management failures discussed in Part VI of this book, funding risk is a contributing cause of the institution's failure. Recall that funding risk is the risk generated by the interaction of liquidity risk and binding trading constraints. This chapter is based on Jarrow [35, 36].

8.1 Set up

For the purposes of this chapter we use a modification of the set up in Chapter 3. We consider a continuous time and finite horizon $[0, T]$ model. The uncertainty is captured by a filtered probability space satisfying the usual conditions $(\Omega, \mathcal{F}, (\mathcal{F}_t), \mathbb{P})$.

We relax the competitive and frictionless market assumptions. Instead, we impose the following assumptions.

Competitive markets.

Competitive means that all traders act as price takers, believing that their trades have no quantity impact on the price.

No transaction costs.

There are no transaction costs, e.g. bid/ask spreads.

Interest rate risk.

Traded is a money market account with initial value $B_0 = 1$ and time t value

$$B_t = e^{\int_0^t r(s)ds} \tag{8.1}$$

where $r(s)$ is the default-free spot rate of interest. This is a stochastic process which is $\mathcal{F}_s$ - measurable.

Risky asset price evolution.

Traded is a risky asset with no cash flows. We assume that the time t price of the risky asset $S_t > 0$ evolves as

$$S_t = S_0 + \int_0^t \mu_S(u)du + \int_0^t \sigma_S(u)dL(u)$$

where $L(t)$ is a Brownian motion under $\mathbb{P}$ with $L(0) = 0$, the drift μ_S and the volatility σ_S are very general stochastic processes depending upon the state of the economy that satisfy the necessary measurability and integrability conditions so that the relevant integrals are well defined.

Over a small time interval $[t, t+\Delta t]$, this expression can be approximated by

$$\triangle S_t = \mu_S(t)\triangle t + \sigma_S(t)\triangle L(t) \tag{8.2}$$

where $\triangle S_t = S_{t+\triangle t} - S_t$ and $\triangle L(t) = L(t + \triangle t) - L(t)$.

The assumption of no cash flows on the risky asset is for simplicity and can easily be relaxed. We consider only one risky asset, but this is also easily extended to many traded risky assets.

Trading constraints are included by assuming that admissible self-financing trading strategies can only lie in a given set K, hence, they are constrained.

Assumption. *(Trading Constraints)*
The admissible self-financing trading strategy must satisfy

$$(\alpha_B(t), \alpha_S(t)) \in K \text{ for all } t$$

where $K \subset \mathbb{R}^2$ is a nonempty, closed, convex cone with $\{(0,0), (1,0), (0,1)\} \subset K$.

Closed means that the set K includes its boundary points. Convex means that if $(\alpha_B^i(t), \alpha_S^i(t)) \in K$ for $i = 1, 2$, then for any $1 > \lambda > 0$, $\lambda(\alpha_B^1(t), \alpha_S^1(t)) + (1 - \lambda)(\alpha_B^2(t), \alpha_S^2(t)) \in K$ as well. And, being a cone means that if $(\alpha_B(t), \alpha_S(t)) \in K$, then $\lambda(\alpha_B(t), \alpha_S(t)) \in K$ for all $\lambda > 0$.

As shown, it is assumed that $\{(0,0),(1,0),(0,1)\} \subset K$. $(0,0) \in K$ implies that no trades satisfy the trading constraint. $\{(1,0),(0,1)\} \subset K$ means that a buy and hold s.f.t.s. involving only the mma, only the risky asset, or (by convex combinations) all of the assets are contained in K.

We denote the trading constrained set of admissible self-financing trading strategies with initial wealth x as:

$$\mathcal{A}(x,K) = \{(\alpha_B(t),\alpha_S(t)) \in K, \ \forall t \in [0,T]\}.$$

The value of the constrained trading strategy $(\alpha_B(t),\alpha_S(t)) \in \mathcal{A}(x,K)$ is

$$X_t^{\alpha_B,\alpha_S} = \alpha_B(t)B_t + \alpha_S(t)S_t \tag{8.3}$$

where $X_0^{\alpha_B,\alpha_S} = x$.

Example. *(Different Trading Constraints)*

This abstract representation of trading constraints is clarified by considering some examples. Fix a time and state, $(t,\omega) \in [0,T] \times \Omega$, and consider a self-financing trading strategy $(\alpha_B(t),\alpha_S(t)) \in \mathbb{R}^2$.

No Trading Constraints.
The case of no constraints is where

$$K = \left\{(\alpha_B,\alpha_S) \in \mathbb{R}^2\right\}.$$

Prohibited Short Sales.
The trading constraint that characterizes a market where there are no short sales is where the risky asset is constrained to be nonnegative. The mma holdings are unrestricted in this market.

$$K = \{(\alpha_B,\alpha_S) \in \mathbb{R}^2 : \alpha_B \in \mathbb{R}, \alpha_S \geq 0\}$$

No Borrowing.
The trading constraint that characterizes a market where there is no borrowing is where the mma is constrained to be nonnegative. The risky asset holdings are unrestricted in this market.

$$K = \{(\alpha_B,\alpha_S) \in \mathbb{R}^2 : \alpha_B \geq 0, \alpha_S \in \mathbb{R}\}$$

Margin Requirements.
This example requires the set $K : [0,T] \times \Omega \to \mathbb{R}^2$ to be a function of (t,ω) which is $\mathcal{F}_t$ - measurable (see Jarrow [36] for the definition of

measurability of a set). The trading constraint that characterizes a market with margin requirements is given by the following set.

$$K = \left\{ (\alpha_B, \alpha_S) \in \mathbb{R}^2 : \alpha_B + \mathfrak{m}\left[(1 + 1_{\alpha_S < 0})\right] S\alpha_S \geq 0 \right\}$$

where S is the risky asset price, $\mathfrak{m} \in [0, 1]$ is the maximum percentage of an asset's wealth that can be borrowed, and $1_{\alpha_S < 0} = \{1$ if $\alpha_S < 0$, 0 otherwise$\}$.

To understand this constraint set, note that if the stock is shorted ($\alpha_S < 0$), then there must be enough funds in the money market account (α_B) to cover $2\mathfrak{m}$ times the value of the short position. This constraint must be satisfied for all times t.

This completes the example.

In an unconstrained market, Chapter 3 defined the notion of an arbitrage opportunity and the notion of NFLVR, i.e. no approximate arbitrage opportunities. In this definition, the admissible self-financing trading strategies are unconstrained. In a market with trading constraints, the analogous notions of an arbitrage opportunity and NFLVR apply, where the definitions apply only to trading strategies in the set $\mathcal{A}(x, K)$. We denote constrained NFLVR as NFLVR_C.

8.2   Results

To price derivatives, we need the following theorem.

Theorem 8.1. *(Sufficient Condition for NFLVR_C)*
Assume there exists a unique local martingale probability $\mathbb{Q}$ equivalent to $\mathbb{P}$.
Then, NFLVR_C is true.

This theorem follows from Chapter 3. The hypothesis implies NFLVR is true for unconstrained self-financing trading strategies. Then, it must also be true for constrained self-financing trading strategies. Hence, NFVLR_C holds.

This theorem assumes that there exists a unique local martingale probability $\mathbb{Q}$. The uniqueness of $\mathbb{Q}$ is important. It implies that, without trading constraints, the market is complete and any derivative's payoff can be constructed synthetically using an admissible self-financing trading strategy. Unfortunately, the trading constraints destroy this market completeness (see the next section).

The content of the theorem is that by assuming the existence of a local martingale probability, this implies that NFLVR_C holds in the market.

Note that this theorem is not an if and only if proposition. For applications, this theorem is sufficient because one normally starts the application by assuming the hypotheses of this theorem, which implies the market satisfies NFLVR_C. This no-arbitrage condition is what is needed for pricing and hedging.

8.3 Pricing and Synthetic Construction

Due to trading constraints, it is easy to see that markets will no longer be complete. This is because trading constraints, when binding, inhibit the construction of a portfolio that matches the payoffs to a traded derivative. This fact implies that we can no longer synthetically construct any derivative's payoff. Hence, there will not be a unique arbitrage-free price for a derivative.

However, we can define upper and lower prices for any derivative. If the derivative's price ever exceeds these bounds, then an arbitrage opportunity exists. The upper price is defined as follows.

Definition 8.2. Given a derivative C_T, the *super-replication price* is defined by

$$\overline{C}_t = inf \left\{ x : \ \exists (\alpha_B(t), \alpha_S(t)) \in \mathcal{A}(x, K) \ s.t. \ X_T^{\alpha_B, \alpha_S} \geq C_T \right\}. \qquad (8.4)$$

The super-replication price corresponds to the smallest amount x one can invest to sell the derivative and pay off the derivative's liabilities with the proceeds from the investment. The lower price is defined analogously.

Definition 8.3. Given a derivative C_T, the *sub-replication price* is defined by

$$\underline{C}_t = sup \left\{ x : \ \exists (\alpha_B(t), \alpha_S(t)) \in \mathcal{A}(x, K) \ s.t. \ X_T^{\alpha_B, \alpha_S} \leq C_T \right\}. \qquad (8.5)$$

The sub-replication price corresponds to the largest amount x one can borrow to buy the derivative and pay off the loan with the proceeds from the derivative.

Given these concepts, we get the following result.

Theorem 8.4. *(Super- and Sub-Replication Prices)*
Assume there exists a unique local martingale probability $\mathbb{Q}$ equivalent to $\mathbb{P}$.

Given a derivative C_T with $E^{\mathbb{Q}}\left(\frac{C_T}{B_T}\right) < \infty$, then

$$\overline{C}_t \geq E^{\mathbb{Q}}\left(\frac{C_T}{B_T} \,|\mathcal{F}_t\right) B_t \geq \underline{C}_t \qquad (8.6)$$

for all t.

For a proof see Jarrow [36], Chapter 21.

To get exact values for $\overline{C}_t, \underline{C}_t$, one needs to solve the optimization problems given in the definitions of the super- and sub-replication prices. This is a difficult exercise that almost always requires a numerical procedure. Similarly, the super- and sub- replication strategies must be obtained numerically as well. Thus, these procedures are not often employed. In practice, due to the complexity of these computations, either trading constraints are ignored or static hedging of derivatives using other traded assets and derivatives is used instead. Static hedging is studied later in the book.

8.4   Bubbles

Since it is only assumed that there exists a local martingale probability $\mathbb{Q}$ in the above theorem, the asset price bubbles discussed in Chapter 3 can exist. It can also be shown that binding trading constraints create another type of asset price bubble, that would otherwise not exist in an unconstrained market (see Jarrow [35]). The intuition for the creation of this asset price bubble is simple. Suppose the trading constraint is that no short sales are allowed. Then a trader, who desires to short sale the asset, will not be able to do so. Consequently, the no short sales constraint is binding to this trader and she sees the market price as overvalued relative to her personalized value. This overvaluation is an asset price bubble to the trader.

Part IV

Optimizing Risk

Overview

There are three entities that we need to understand how to risk manage their assets, liabilities, and cash flows: individuals, firms, and banks. The difference between firms and banks is that banks are regulated, which imposes a capital constraint on a bank's activities that firms do not have. For the health of the financial system, regulators impose constraints on a bank's capital to avoid externality costs caused by the bank's failure on financial markets. To understand these externality costs, note that when banks fail, individuals' and firms' consumption and production activities, respectively, are inhibited. These create costs to these entities not borne by the banks. By internalizing these costly externalities to the bank, the bank's decisions will be modified to be more consistent with society's welfare.

Conceptually, once we determine the objective of each of these entities, the risk management problem is solved when the entity chooses an optimal portfolio to maximize their objective function subject to any relevant constraints. This decision problem involves stochastic dynamic programming. There are two cases to be considered.

Global Risk Management

The problem of optimizing the risk in a portfolio or balance sheet can be thought of as the *global* (overall) risk management problem. The word "global" capturing the ability to solve the entire dynamic stochastic control problem over the entity's life. Needless to say, global risk management is hard to do in practice since it requires significant information on preferences, asset dynamics, and market structures. All of these are difficult, if not impossible, to obtain in their entirety. In addition, even if this structure was knowable, the complexity and size of the resulting problem makes the determination of a realistic solution to the problem an impossible task.

Local Risk Management

In this part of the book we study the global risk management problem for conceptual understanding. In contrast, what happens in practice can better be described as *local* risk management. This is risk management performed by decomposing the global risk management problem into smaller parts and managing the risks of these smaller parts. Of course, the hope is that by managing the risks of the smaller parts, the overall risk management implied by this approach approximates that from the global risk management solution.

Chapter 9

Individuals

This chapter studies an individual's risk management problem with respect to their investment portfolio.

9.1   Set up

We discuss an individual's portfolio problem using the simple economy from Chapter 3. The economy is frictionless and competitive. We consider a continuous time and finite horizon $[0, T]$ model. The uncertainty is captured by a filtered probability space satisfying the usual conditions $(\Omega, \mathcal{F}, (\mathcal{F}_t), \mathbb{P})$. Recall that traded are a money market account $B_t = e^{rt}$ and a risky asset S_t with no cash flows. A trading strategy is a pair of holdings in these assets $(\alpha_B(t), \alpha_S(t))$ for all t and ω with initial wealth $X_0 = x$ and time t value $X_t = \alpha_B(t)B_t + \alpha_S(t)S_t$. Let $\mathcal{A}(x)$ be the set of all admissible self-financing trading strategies starting with initial wealth x. The assumption of a single risky asset with no cash flows is used to simplify the presentation. This assumption is easily relaxed, but since it introduces only more complex notation and no additional insights, this generalization is not provided herein.

9.2   Objective

This section quantifies an individual's preferences or objective function. Let us suppose that the individual has beliefs $\mathbb{P}$ and needs to choose an element from the space of nonnegative random variables at time T denoted $C \in \mathcal{L}_+^0$. This is the set of possible time T wealths. Note that in the previous chapters we called this the space of derivatives. This set includes the payoffs to the money market account and the risky asset.

9.2.1 The Expected Utility Hypothesis

To construct the objective function, we need to transform the choice space from the set of random wealths to the set of probability distributions over the nonnegative real numbers, $\mathbb{R}_+$. A probability distribution on $\mathbb{R}_+$ is a function $P : \mathbb{R}_+ \rightarrow [0,1]$ which is nondecreasing with $P(0) = 0$ and $\lim_{z \to \infty} P(z) = 1$. Each $C \in \mathcal{L}_+^0$ generates a probability distribution in the following manner. Given $C \in \mathcal{L}_+^0$, define

$$P_C(z) = \mathbb{P}(C(\omega) \leq z)$$

for all $z \geq 0$.

Define $\mathcal{B}$ to be the set of all probability distributions over $\mathbb{R}_+$. Note that the probability distribution with $\{x\}$ occurring with probability one is in this set, i.e. $\delta_x \in \mathcal{B}$ where $\delta_x(y) \equiv \{0 \text{ if } y < x, \ 1 \text{ if } x \leq y\}$ for $y \in \mathbb{R}_+$.

We assume that the individual has a preference relation $\succsim$ over the set $\mathcal{B}$. If $P_1 \succsim P_2$, then P_1 is preferred or indifferent to P_2. We define indifference $\sim$ as $P_1 \sim P_2$ if and only $P_1 \succsim P_2$ and $P_2 \succsim P_1$. We define strict preference $\succ$ as $P_1 \succ P_2$ if and only if $P_1 \succsim P_2$ and not $P_1 \sim P_2$. We assume that these preferences satisfy the following rationality axioms.

1. *Reflexivity:* For any $P \in \mathcal{B}$, $P \succsim P$.

2. *Comparability:* For any $P_1, P_2 \in \mathcal{B}$, either $P_1 \succsim P_2$ or $P_2 \succsim P_1$.

3. *Transitivity:* For any $P_1, P_2, P_3 \in \mathcal{B}$, if $P_1 \succsim P_2$ and $P_2 \succsim P_3$, then $P_1 \succsim P_3$.

4. *Order Preserving:* For any $P_1, P_2 \in \mathcal{B}$ where $P_1 \succ P_2$ and $p_1, p_2 \in [0,1]$, $[p_1 P_1 + (1 - p_1)P_2] \succ [p_2 P_1 + (1 - p_2)P_2]$ if and only if $p_1 > p_2$.

5. *Intermediate Value:* For any $P_1, P_2, P_3 \in \mathcal{B}$, if $P_1 \succ P_2 \succ P_3$ then there exists a unique $p \in (0,1)$ such that $P_2 \sim pP_1 + (1 - p)P_3$.

6. *Boundedness:* There exist $P_U, P_L \in \mathcal{B}$ such that $P_U \succsim P \succsim P_L$ for all $P \in \mathcal{B}$.

7. *Strong Independence:* For any $P_1, P_2 \in \mathcal{B}$, if $P_1 \succ P_2$ then for any $p \in (0,1)$ and any $P \in \mathcal{B}$, $pP_1 + (1 - p)P \succ pP_2 + (1 - p)P$.

If the individual satisfies these axioms, then the following theorem holds.

Theorem 9.1. *(Linear Utility) If these 7 axioms are satisfied, then there exists a utility function* $\mathscr{U} : \mathscr{B} \to \mathbb{R}$ *such that given* $P_1, P_2 \in \mathscr{B}$,

$$P_1 \succsim P_2 \quad \text{if and only if} \quad \mathscr{U}(P_1) \geq \mathscr{U}(P_2)$$

and

$$\mathscr{U}(pP_1 + (1-p)P_2) = p\mathscr{U}(P_1) + (1-p)\mathscr{U}(P_2).$$

For a proof see Jarrow [24].

We assume that our individual satisfies all of these rationality axioms. The study of finance under an alternative set of axioms which violate rationality is called behavioral finance.

Remark. (Behavioral Finance)
Behavioral finance studies financial markets when individuals do not satisfy these rationality axioms. Of the rationality axioms stated above, the strong independence axiom is the rationality axiom that is most often violated by participants in laboratory experiments. Because of this and other evidence, many scholars believe that individuals do not satisfy these rationality axioms. For a survey of this literature see Barberis and Thaler [4]. This completes the remark.

Given an individual with preferences $\succsim$ over $P \in \mathscr{B}$, we assume in addition that $\succeq$ is continuous relative to convergence in distributions (the weak convergence topology on $\mathscr{B}$ (see Ash [2], p. 199)). Define a "new" utility function $U : \mathbb{R}_+ \to \mathbb{R}$, over the certain outcomes $\{x\} \in \mathbb{R}_+$, by $U(x) \equiv \mathscr{U}(\delta_x)$. Then, it can be shown (see Jarrow [24]) using the linearity of $\mathscr{U}$ that the individual's preferences over $P \in \mathscr{B}$ can be written as an expected utility, i.e.

$$\mathscr{U}(P) = \mathcal{E}^P(U(x))$$

where $\mathcal{E}^P(\cdot)$ is expectation using $P \in \mathscr{B}$.

Finally, using the equivalence between a $P_C \in \mathscr{B}$ and a $C \in \mathcal{L}^0_+$ for fixed beliefs $\mathbb{P}$, we can write (see Ash [2], p. 223) the individual's objective function as

$$\mathscr{U}(P_C) = \mathcal{E}^{P_C}(U(x)) = E(U(C)).$$

9.2.2 Risk Aversion

Also needed for our subsequent discussion is a notion of risk aversion. This is provided in the following definition.

Definition 9.2. *(Risk Aversion)* Given a $C \in \mathcal{L}_+^0$, we say that an individual is

$$
\begin{array}{lll}
\text{risk averse} & \text{if} & U(E(C)) > E(U(C)) \\
\text{risk neutral} & \text{if} & U(E(C)) = E(U(C)) \\
\text{risk loving} & \text{if} & U(E(C)) < E(U(C))
\end{array}
$$

An individual is risk averse if she prefers receiving the expected value of a gamble to playing the gamble. An individual is risk neutral if she is indifferent between receiving the expected value of a gamble and playing the gamble. And, an individual is risk loving if she prefers playing the gamble instead of receiving the expected value of the gamble.

If an individual's utility function is concave, then by Jensen's inequality, the individual is risk averse. For the subsequent analysis we assume that an individual's utility function is concave and thus they are risk averse.

9.2.3 The Risk Management Problem

Consequently, under the above assumptions, the individual's risk management problem can be written as:

$$
\max_{(\alpha_B, \alpha_S) \in \mathcal{A}(x)} E\left(U(\alpha_B(T)B_T + \alpha_S(t)S_T)\right). \tag{9.1}
$$

The goal of the investor is to choose an admissible self-financing trading strategy $(\alpha_B, \alpha_S) \in \mathcal{A}(x)$ that maximizes the expected utility of terminal wealth $X_T = \alpha_B(T)B_T + \alpha_S(T)S_T$.

To facilitate the existence of a solution to expression (9.1), we also assume that the individual's utility function satisfies an additional regularity property known as *reasonable asymptotic elasticity*. Assuming that U is twice differentiable and that $\lim_{z \to \infty} \left(\frac{-zU''(z)}{U'(z)}\right)$ exists, the condition is that $\lim_{z \to \infty} \left(\frac{-zU''(z)}{U'(z)}\right) > 0$ (see Schachermayer [53]). It can be shown that a solution exists to expression (9.1) under the above structure if the market satisfies NFLVR (see Pham [54], Chapter 7).

9.3 Solution

There are two possibilities for the solution to problem (9.1). The two cases correspond to whether the market satisfies NFLVR or not. If there exists an approximate arbitrage opportunity (NFLVR is violated), then there exists a sequence of trading strategies that generates unbounded expected utility. These trading strategies correspond to the approximate arbitrage opportunities. If NFVLR is satisfied, then an optimal trading strategy or portfolio across time $(\alpha_B, \alpha_S) \in \mathcal{A}(x)$ exists. Such a trading strategy solves the investor's risk management problem.

Hence, the optimal portfolio selection can be decomposed into two tasks. The first task is to search for and exploit any mispriced securities. These do not exist if the markets satisfy NFLVR. After the first task is completed, the second task is to choose a risk-optimized (efficient) portfolio. We discuss each of these tasks in turn.

9.3.1   Finding Arbitrage Opportunities

This section discusses how to identify mispriced securities to exploit in a portfolio. The procedure is based on fitting a multiple-factor model to a risky asset's historical returns to see if it has a non-zero "alpha." To understand this procedure, we need to derive a multiple-factor model for any risky asset's return.

It can be shown that under NFLVR and ND (see Jarrow and Protter [40]), given the return on any asset $R_S(t) = \frac{S(t+t\triangle)-S(t)}{S(t)}$ over a time period $[t, t + \triangle t]$, there exists a collection of risk-factor returns denoted $r_j(t)$ for $j \in J$ such that

$$R_S(t) = r_0(t) + \sum_{j \in J_S} \beta_{S\,j}(t)\,(r_j(t) - r_0(t)) + \varepsilon_S(t) \qquad (9.2)$$

where $r_0(t)$ is the default-free spot rate of interest over $[t, t+\triangle t]$, $\beta_{S\,j}(t) \neq 0$ is the asset's beta with respect to the jth risk-factor for a finite set of risk-factors specific to the asset S, i.e. J_S, and $\varepsilon_S(t)$ is a residual with $E\left(\varepsilon_S(t)\,|\mathcal{F}_t\right) = 0$. This is true for all traded assets S. The risk-factors are traded portfolios. They are called risk-factors because they reflect the common randomness in asset prices across the economy, called *systematic risk*, with nonzero risk premiums, i.e. $E\left(r_j(t) - r_0(t)\,|\mathcal{F}_t\right) \neq 0$. Expression (9.2) is called a *multiple-factor model*.

Assuming ND holds, an NFLVR can be determined by fitting a modification of expression (9.2) to historical return data. The modification is to add a constant alpha to this expression as in

$$R_S(t) = \alpha_S + r_0(t) + \sum_{j \in J_S} \beta_{S\,j}(t)\,(r_j(t) - r_0(t)) + \varepsilon_S(t). \qquad (9.3)$$

This constant alpha α_S is known as *Jensen's alpha*. If in the empirical estimation $\alpha_S \neq 0$, then a NFLVR exists.

The rule for buying/selling the risky asset is that if $\alpha_S > 0$, then buy the security. If $\alpha_S < 0$, then short the security. Of course, this approach can also be applied to the returns on trading strategies. If a trading strategy has a positive alpha, then the trading strategy is an approximate arbitrage opportunity. The search for positive alpha trading strategies is the basis for active portfolio management (see Jarrow [31]). If one does not assume ND holds, then the above procedure can be generalized to include the existence of asset price bubbles in expression (9.2) as well, see Jarrow [34].

9.3.2   Risk Optimized Portfolios

If the market satisfies NFLVR, then there are no mispriced securities, and the task for the individual trader is to find the portfolio to maximize their expected utility, i.e. to implement the solution to problem (9.1). This yields a risk optimized or efficient portfolio.

Determining the optimal portfolio requires solving the stochastic dynamic portfolio problem, which is a non-trivial exercise for any realistic modeling of the economy (for the mathematics of this approach see Pham [54]). Although we will not pursue the solution procedure in this book, an important example that is often used in practice clarifies this discussion.

Example. *(Mean-Variance Utility)*
    The simplest example is when an individual has a mean-variance utility of wealth function:

$$U(X) = E(X) - b \cdot Var(X)$$

for $b > 0$.
    Let's consider a static problem with only two time periods $t = 0$ and $t = T$. Substituting the mean-variance utility function into expression (9.1), one can show that the optimal portfolio solves the simpler problem

$$\min_{(\alpha_B,\alpha_S)\in\mathcal{A}(x)} Var(X_T) \quad s.t. \atop E(X_T) = \mu > 0 \tag{9.4}$$

where μ is chosen based on the risk aversion parameter b.
    The solution to the individual' optimization problem, the optimal portfolio, has minimum variance for a given expected return μ. Expression (9.4) is a quadratic programming problem, and its solution is well studied (see Back [3]). The optimal portfolio $(\alpha_B, \alpha_S) \in \mathcal{A}(x)$ solving this problem is called an *efficient portfolio*. This simpler problem is often followed by financial institutions when forming investment portfolios. This completes the example.

9.4 Complications

In practice, one needs to generalize this model to include: (i) more assets, including cash flows on the assets, (ii) more complex preferences including preferences over consumption at intermediate dates, (iii) market frictions including trading constraints and transaction costs, and (iv) liquidity risk - a quantity impact on the price. As evidenced by this list of extensions, determining the global solution to the investor's risk management problem under these more realistic assumptions and structures on the economy is an impossible task. Consequently, we will be content with the simpler problem of understanding how to risk manage a subset of the investor's portfolio given a particular pre-specified purpose. An example might be that the individual wants to cap the interest rate paid on an existing floating rate loan held in their portfolio. Alternatively, the individual may want to eliminate foreign currency exchange rate risk from their investment portfolio. We call this *local* risk management. This discussion is pursued in Part V of the book.

Chapter 10

Firms

This chapter studies a firm's risk management problem. To illustrate the issues involved we discuss a firm's risk management problem using the simple economy from Chapter 3. A *firm* is defined to be any corporation whose equity capital is not constrained by bank regulators. If a corporation's capital is constrained by bank regulators, it is called a *bank* and not a firm.

10.1 Set up

The economy is assumed to be frictionless and competitive. We consider a continuous time and finite horizon $[0, T]$ model. The uncertainty is captured by a filtered probability space satisfying the usual conditions $(\Omega, \mathcal{F}, (\mathcal{F}_t), \mathbb{P})$.

Recall that traded are a money market account $B_t = e^{rt}$ and a risky asset S_t. A trading strategy is a pair of holdings in these assets $(\alpha_B(t), \alpha_S(t))$ for all t and ω with initial wealth $X_0 = x$ and time t value $X_t = \alpha_B(t)B_t + \alpha_S(t)S_t$. Let $\mathcal{A}(x)$ be the set of all admissible self-financing trading strategies starting with initial wealth x.

When discussing a firm, we can interpret a trading strategy as choosing a collection of investment projects. Shorting the money market account corresponds to borrowing (choosing a liability) and buying the risky asset is interpreted as investing in a project, e.g. producing widgets.

10.2 Objective

The firm is owned by a set of shareholders and run by a management team. The firm's actions reflect the collective set of shareholder preferences over the time T value of the firm's wealth, which in this case is the firm's equity value. If the firm's actions reflect preferences that exhibit risk aversion and rationality, then the firm's objective can be characterized as being an expected utility function. In this case, solving the firm's risk management problem is equivalent to solving the investor's portfolio problem and the discussion from Chapter 9 applies.

However, firms are typically thought of as being risk neutral with the objective of maximizing the value of the shareholder's equity. In our simplified economy, this is equivalent to solving the following problem

$$\max_{(\alpha_B, \alpha_S) \in \mathcal{A}(x)} E\left(\alpha_B(T)e^{rT} + \alpha_S(T)S_T\right)e^{-rT}. \tag{10.1}$$

The objective in this expression is the expected discounted (e^{-rT}) value of the firm's terminal equity $(\alpha_B(T)e^{rT} + \alpha_S(T)S_T)$, or equivalently, the present value of shareholder's wealth.

10.3   Solution

As in the previous chapter, there are two possibilities for the solution to problem (10.1). The two cases correspond to whether the market satisfies NFLVR or not. If there exists an approximate arbitrage opportunity (NFLVR is violated), then there exists a sequence of trading strategies that generates unbounded expected wealth. These trading strategies correspond to the approximate arbitrage opportunities.

If NFVLR is satisfied, then an optimal solution exists and the shareholders' wealth is finite. In this later case, the optimal solution is to choose those projects with the highest expected return, until the initial wealth (capital) is depleted. It is important to note that in a competitive and frictionless markets, there is a separation of the firms investment (α_S) and financing (α_B) decisions. Hence, because the firm can borrow in unlimited amounts, the firm should choose all net present value (NPV) > 0 projects, until no NPV > 0 projects remain. This is the standard capital budgeting methodology taught in corporate finance courses (see Brealey, Myers, Allen [7]).

Example. *(Finding Arbitrage Opportunities)*
Suppose the market does not satisfy NFLVR, i.e. there exist approximate arbitrage opportunities. Consider a financial institution seeking investment opportunities among traded financial securities. This could be a hedge fund or mutual fund. Note that under our definition of a firm, these are not banks because their capital is not subject to regulatory constraints. When considering investment opportunities among traded financial securities the use of Jensen's alpha is a useful tool.

As discussed in Chapter 9, if NFLVR and ND hold, then for the return on any asset $R_S(t)$ over the time interval $[t, t+\triangle t]$, there exists a collection of risk-factor returns denoted $r_j(t)$ for $j \in J$ such that

$$R_S(t) = r_0(t) + \sum_{j \in J_S} \beta_{S\,j}(t)\,(r_j(t) - r_0(t)) + \varepsilon_S(t) \tag{10.2}$$

where $r_0(t)$ is the default-free spot rate of interest over $[t, t+\triangle t]$, $\beta_{S\,j}(t) \neq 0$ is the asset's beta with respect to the jth risk-factor for a set of risk-factors specific to the asset S, i.e. J_S, and $\varepsilon_S(t)$ is a residual with $E\,(\varepsilon_S(t)\,|\mathcal{F}_t) = 0$. This is true for all traded assets S. The risk-factors are traded portfolios that reflect systematic risk in the economy.

Assuming ND holds, an NFLVR can be determined by fitting the following expression to historical return data. This expression adds a constant alpha to the multiple-factor model, i.e.

$$R_S(t) = \alpha_S + r_0(t) + \sum_{j \in J_S} \beta_{S\,j}(t)\,(r_j(t) - r_0(t)) + \varepsilon_S(t). \tag{10.3}$$

If $\alpha_S \neq 0$, then a NFLVR exists. The rule for buying/selling assets is that if $\alpha_S > 0$, then buy the security. If $\alpha_S < 0$, then short the security. This completes the example.

10.4 Complications

Of course, in practice there are market frictions and trading constraints. A market friction might be bankruptcy costs. A trading constraint might be restrictions on the magnitude of a firm's borrowings due to asymmetric information. These frictions invalidate the NPV > 0 rule discussed above, and the firm's investment and financing decisions can no longer be separated. These frictions complicate the firm's risk management problem whose solution, in this case, is obtained by solving expression (10.1) subject to the market frictions and trading constraints.

As with the individual's risk management problem, determining the global solution to the firm's risk management problem under realistic assumptions and structures on the economy is also an impossible task. Consequently, we must again be content with understanding the simpler problem of how to risk manage a subset of the firm's investment projects given a particular pre-specified purpose. An example might be to hedge the foreign exchange exposure of the firm's product sales in foreign countries. We call this *local* risk management. This discussion is pursued in Part V of this book.

Chapter 11

Banks

This chapter discusses a bank's risk management problem. As before, to illustrate the issues involved we discuss a bank's risk management problem using the simple economy from Chapter 3.

11.1 Set up

The economy is frictionless and competitive. We consider a continuous time and finite time $[0, T]$ model. The uncertainty is captured by a filtered probability space satisfying the usual conditions $(\Omega, \mathcal{F}, (\mathcal{F}_t), \mathbb{P})$. Recall that traded are a money market account $B_t = e^{rt}$ and a risky asset S_t. A trading strategy is a pair of holdings in these assets $(\alpha_B(t), \alpha_S(t))$ for all t and ω with initial wealth $X_0 = x$ and time t value $X_t = \alpha_B(t)B_t + \alpha_S(t)S_t$. Let $\mathcal{A}(x)$ be the set of all admissible self-financing trading strategies starting with initial wealth x.

When discussing a bank, we can interpret a trading strategy as choosing a collection of assets and liabilities. Shorting the money market account can correspond to borrowing (choosing a liability) and buying the risky asset is interpreted as making a loan or purchasing a bond.

11.2 Objective

The bank's objective is analogous that that of a firm. Following the discussion is Chapter 10, if the bank's actions reflect preferences that exhibit risk aversion and rationality, then the bank's objective function can be characterized as being an expected utility function. In this case, solving the bank's risk management problem is equivalent to solving the investor's portfolio problem and the discussion from Chapter 9 applies with the modification noted below relating to regulatory constraints.

However, banks are typically thought of as being risk neutral with the objective of maximizing the value of the shareholder's equity. Unlike firms, banks are monitored by financial regulators. For the health of the financial system, regulators impose a constraint on the bank's capital to avoid externality costs caused by the bank's failure on financial markets. To understand these externality costs, note that when banks fail, individuals' and firms' consumption and production activities, respectively, are inhibited. These create costs to these entities not borne by the banks. By internalizing these costly externalities to the bank, the bank's decisions will be modified to be more consistent with society's welfare.

These externality costs are also related to the notion of *systemic risk*, which by definition is the risk to asset prices generated by the failure of well-functioning financial markets. If enough banks fail in an economy, this could in turn cause the failure of the financial system. The externality costs due to systemic risk are also included in the determination of a bank's regulatory capital.

11.2.1   Regulatory Risk Measures

To understand the constraints on capital imposed by regulators, we need to first understand the notion of a regulatory risk measure. A *regulatory risk measure* is a function ρ that quantifies the risk of a bank's *change in equity value* over some future time interval $[0, T]$. The change in equity value C is an element of the set of random variables $\mathcal{L}^0$.

There are many different regulatory risk measures. We discuss three of these: coherent risk measures, value-at-risk, and the insurance value of the bank. A *coherent risk* measure is any risk measure that satisfies the following four axioms.

1. *(Translation invariance)* Given $C \in \mathcal{L}^0$ and $\alpha > 0$, $\rho(C + \alpha) = \rho(C) - \alpha$.

2. *(Positive homogeneity)* Given $C \in \mathcal{L}^0$ and $\lambda > 0$, $\rho(\lambda C) = \lambda \rho(C)$.

3. *(Subadditivity (diversification))* Given $C_1, C_2 \in \mathcal{L}^0$, $\rho(C_1 + C_2) \leq \rho(C_1) + \rho(C_2)$.

4. *(Monotonicity)* Given $C_1 \leq C_2$, $\rho(C_1) \leq \rho(C_2)$.

As axioms, the truth of these conditions should be self-evident. The translation invariance axiom says that if one adds α dollars of capital to the bank, the risk measure should decline by α dollars. This makes the risk measure the same scale as dollars. Positive homogeneity is another axiom that makes the risk measure scale to dollars. The subadditivity axiom captures the benefits of diversification. It says that the risk of two banks combined is less than or equal to the risk of the two banks considered separately. Last, monotonicity says that if bank 1's time T change in equity is always less than bank 2's time T change in equity, then the risk of bank 1 is less than the risk of bank 2.

Another well-known regulatory risk measure is *value-at-risk (VaR)*. VaR is defined by the following expression:

$$VaR_\alpha(C) = sup\{x : \mathbb{P}(C \leq x) \leq \alpha\}.$$

VaR is that quantity of capital x for which the change in equity value occurs less than or equal to x with probability α. Alternatively stated, it is that change in equity value x for which worse losses occur only with probability α (see Jorion [47, 48]). It is known that VaR satisfies axioms 1, 2, 4 above, but violates the diversification axiom 3, see Jarrow and Chatterjea [37], p. 751. Hence, VaR is not a coherent risk measure. The fact that VaR violates the diversification axiom is viewed as a serious deficiency of VaR as a regulatory risk measure. A second deficiency is that it ignores the magnitude of equity losses below the VaR level.

Other risk measures exist, one is related to the cost of insuring against the bank's insolvency. This is the value of a put option with strike 0 written on the firm's equity value losses C over the life of the bank $[0, T]$, i.e.

$$\rho(C) = E^{\mathbb{Q}} \left(\frac{max[-C, 0]}{B_T} \right)$$

where $\mathbb{Q}$ is the risk-neutral probability, which exists if markets satisfy NFLVR and ND. Note that C corresponds to the change in equity value over $[0, T]$, hence, $-C$ corresponds to the loss in equity value over $[0, T]$, but denoted as a positive quantity. This insurance value risk measure satisfies axioms 2 - 4, but it is also not a coherent risk measure because it violates the translation invariance axiom 1, see Jarrow [27].

11.2.2 The Constrained Optimization Problem

We assume that the regulator selects a risk measure $\rho(C)$ for $C \in \mathcal{L}^0$. In practice, the regulators often use multiple risk measures, one of which is VaR. Given that the regulator's impose a risk constraint on the bank's equity capital, the bank's risk management problem becomes

$$\max_{(\alpha_B, \alpha_S) \in \mathcal{A}(x)} E \left((\alpha_B(T)e^{rT} + \alpha_S(T)S_T) \right) e^{-rT} \quad s.t.$$
$$\rho([\alpha_B(T)e^{rT} + \alpha_S(T)S_T] - [\alpha_B(0) + \alpha_S(0)S_0]) \leq \delta \quad (11.1)$$

for some $\delta > 0$.

The objective in this expression is the expected discounted value of the bank's terminal equity value, or equivalently, the present value of shareholder's wealth. The constraint requires that the bank's regulatory risk measure of the change in the equity's value over $[0, T]$ must be less than or equal to δ.

11.3   Solution

As in the previous chapter, there are two possibilities for the solution to problem (11.1). The two cases correspond to whether the market satisfies NFLVR or not. If there exists an approximate arbitrage opportunity (NFLVR is violated), then there exists a sequence of trading strategies that generates unbounded expected wealth. These trading strategies correspond to the approximate arbitrage opportunities. Because unbounded expected wealth is generated, the regulatory risk constraint will be non-binding and satisfied by these approximate arbitrage opportunities.

If NFVLR is satisfied, then an optimal solution exists and the shareholders' wealth is finite. The constraint in the risk management problem implies that there is *not* a separation of the bank's investment and financing decisions. A net present value (NPV) > 0 rule still applies, but it needs to be modified for the opportunity cost of the bank's regulatory constraint. Intuitively, the discount rate needs to be increased by this opportunity cost (see Jarrow and Purnanandam [41] and Broadie, Cvitanic, and Soner [8]). The exact magnitude of the discount rate increase requires the solution to the bank's risk management problem (11.1). Unfortunately, there are no commonly accepted models in this regard.

Example. *(Finding Arbitrage Opportunities)*

Analogous to firms, suppose the market does not satisfy NFLVR, i.e. there exist approximate arbitrage opportunities. When considering investment opportunities among traded financial securities the use of Jensen's alpha is a useful tool.

As discussed in Chapter 9, if NFLVR and ND hold, then for the return on any asset $R_S(t)$ over the time interval $[t, t + \triangle t]$, there exists a collection of risk-factor returns denoted $r_j(t)$ for $j \in J$ such that

$$R_S(t) = r_0(t) + \sum_{j \in J_S} \beta_{S\,j}(t)\,(r_j(t) - r_0(t)) + \varepsilon_S(t) \qquad (11.2)$$

where $r_0(t)$ is the default-free spot rate of interest over $[t, t + \triangle t]$, $\beta_{S\,j}(t) \neq 0$ is the asset's beta with respect to the jth risk-factor for a set of risk-factors specific to the asset S, i.e. J_S, and $\varepsilon_S(t)$ is a residual with $E\left(\varepsilon_S(t)\,|\mathcal{F}_t\right) = 0$. This is true for all traded assets S. The risk-factors are traded portfolios that reflect systematic risk in the economy.

Assuming ND holds, an NFLVR can be determined by fitting the following expression to historical return data. This expression adds a constant alpha to the multiple-factor model, i.e.

$$R_S(t) = \alpha_S + r_0(t) + \sum_{j \in J_S} \beta_{S\,j}(t)\left(r_j(t) - r_0(t)\right) + \varepsilon_S(t).$$

If $\alpha_S \neq 0$, then a NFLVR exists.

In contrast to firms, given the capital constraint, an $\alpha_S > 0$ is not sufficient to buy the asset. It must earn an additional premium to cover the opportunity cost of the additional equity capital. Determining the magnitude of this premium requires computing the solution to the bank's risk management problem (11.1). This completes the example.

11.4 Complications

Of course, in practice there are also market frictions and additional trading constraints. A market friction might be bankruptcy costs. A trading constraint might be restrictions on the magnitude of bank's borrowings from other financial institutions due to asymmetric information. In these circumstances, capital is often further restricted. Here, the risk management of the bank's cash flows and assets become an important consideration. Risk management is performed to maximize shareholder's wealth subject to the market frictions, trading constraints, and regulatory restrictions.

As with the firm's risk management problem, determining the global solution to the bank's risk management problem under realistic assumptions and structures on the economy is an impossible task. Consequently, we must be content with understanding the simpler problem of how to risk manage a subset of the bank's investment projects given a particular prespecified purpose. An example might be to hedge the credit default swap exposure in the bank's swap book. We call this *local* risk management. This discussion is pursued in Part V below.

Part V

Managing Risks

Overview

This part of the book concentrates on the local management of risks, as opposed to global risk management, which is too hard to do in practice and discussed in Part IV of this book. We have already discussed capital budgeting in Part IV (the finding and taking advantage of NPV > 0 opportunities). We now focus on a different question. Given the balance sheet of a firm or bank (after the capital budgeting selections) or the investment portfolio of an individual, how to manage its risk profile.

There are two basic approaches to local risk management. The first is using diversification to reduce risk. The second is to buy insurance, or equivalently, hedge to reduce risk. When hedging, one can directly purchase the insurance. This is called static hedging. Or, one can synthetically construct the insurance by trading in the primary securities. This is called dynamic hedging. We discuss all of these methods below.

Chapter 12

Diversification

This chapter discusses the importance of diversification in risk management.

12.1 The Basic Idea

When holding a large collection of assets in a portfolio or balance sheet, diversification is a powerful tool to control risk. The idea is very simple, consider the returns on two assets r_1, r_2 over some time period $[0, T]$. Suppose these assets are held in a portfolio with weights $w_1, w_2 \geq 0$ where $w_1 + w_2 = 1$. Then, the return on the portfolio is

$$R = w_1 r_1 + w_2 r_2. \tag{12.1}$$

The expected return and variance of the portfolio are easily computed.

$$E(R) = w_1 E(r_1) + w_2 E(r_2)$$
$$\sigma^2(R) = w_1^2 \sigma^2(r_1) + 2w_1 w_2 corr(r_1, r_2)\sigma(r_1)\sigma(r_2) + w_2^2 \sigma^2(r_2) \tag{12.2}$$
$$= (w_1\sigma(r_1) + w_2\sigma(r_1))^2 + 2w_1 w_2[corr(r_1, r_2) - 1]\sigma(r_1)\sigma(r_2)$$

where $corr(\cdot, \cdot)$ is correlation and $\sigma^2(\cdot)$ is variance.

To understand the power of diversification, suppose that the two assets have identical expected returns and variances, which are given by $E(r), \sigma^2(r)$. Then, the portfolio's characteristics are:

$$E(R) = E(r)$$
$$\sigma^2(R) = \sigma^2(r) + 2w_1 w_2[corr(r_1, r_2) - 1]\sigma^2(r) \tag{12.3}$$

In this case, the portfolio has the same expected return as each individual asset, but its variance is different.

If the correlation between the asset's returns is perfect, i.e. $corr(r_1, r_2) = 1$, then the variance of the portfolio is equal to the variance of a single asset. No risk reduction is obtained. In fact, if the correlation is perfect, they are the same asset (just with different names).

If the correlation between the asset's return is strictly less than one, i.e. $corr(r_1, r_2) < 1$, then the variance of the portfolio is strictly less than the individual asset's variance. This is the effect of diversification. In fact, if the correlation between the returns of the two assets is negative, the effect of diversification is even more powerful.

It is interesting to note that in the extreme case that the asset returns are perfectly negatively correlated, $corr(r_1, r_2) = -1$, then one can construct a riskless portfolio using these two assets. Indeed, to do this just set the holdings in each asset to have equal weights, i.e. $w_1 = w_2 = \frac{1}{2}$. Then simple algebra shows that the variance of the portfolio is 0. This is the idea behind the synthetic construction of a derivative security to create arbitrage or to completely remove the risk from a traded derivative position.

12.2   Portfolio Risk Minimization

An important example of the power of diversification, often used in practice, is when a financial institution constructs a portfolio to minimize its variance for a given expected return. We discussed such a portfolio in the context of an individual's risk management problem in Chapter 9.

To illustrate this optimization problem, consider a portfolio consisting of n assets with returns $r_1, \ldots, r_n$ over some time period $[0, T]$. Consider an arbitrary portfolio with weights $w_1, \ldots, w_n$ where $w_1 + \cdots + w_n = 1$. The return on this portfolio is

$$R = \sum_{i=1}^{n} w_i r_i. \tag{12.4}$$

The portfolio's expected return and variance are:

$$E(R) = \sum_{i=1}^{n} w_i E(r_i)$$
$$\sigma^2(R) = \sum_{i=1}^{n} \sum_{j=1}^{n} w_i w_j corr(r_i, r_j) \sigma(r_i) \sigma(r_j) \tag{12.5}$$

The portfolio risk minimization problem is

$$\min_{(w_1, \cdots, w_n)} \sigma^2(R) \quad s.t.$$
$$E(R) = \mu > 0 \tag{12.6}$$
$$\sum_{i=1}^{n} w_i = 1$$

This is a quadratic optimization whose solution is well understood. Software packages are readily available to numerically solve this optimization problem (see Boyd and Vandenberghe [6], Chapter 4).

12.3 Conclusion

Diversification is a powerful tool that can be used in risk management to reduce the variance (risk) of a portfolio or balance sheet. Applying this notion quantitatively is often a difficult exercise, except when: (i) doing portfolio risk minimization as just discussed in the previous section as a quadratic programming problem, or (ii) when eliminating risk via the use of dynamic or static hedging, as discussed in the next two chapters. Nonetheless, it is regularly employed in practice at an intuitive level in the daily management of a firm's assets or an individual's portfolio.

Chapter 13

Static Hedging

Static hedging is the reduction in a portfolio's risk by using buy and hold trading strategies composed of existing traded assets and derivatives. Static hedging can also sometimes be used to synthetically construct derivatives and identify arbitrage opportunities. This section illustrates risk management using static hedging by studying various examples.

We assume frictionless and competitive markets in this chapter. Frictionless means that there are no transactions costs and no trading constraints, e.g. short sale constraints or margin requirements. Competitive means that all traders act as price takers, believing that there trades have no quantity impact on the price.

13.1 Risk Reduction

This section discusses how derivatives can be used to reduce the risk of an existing portfolio by studying a few examples. This is just the proverbial "tip of the iceberg."

13.1.1 Portfolio Insurance

European put options can be used to reduce the risk on an equity portfolio. Consider an equity portfolio with time t value S_t.

Suppose the portfolio has done well, and one wants to lock in the gains over $[0, \tau]$ without selling the portfolio. To do this, one can buy a European put option on the portfolio with strike price $K = S_t$ and maturity τ. This derivative locks in the S_t value until time τ.

To see this note that the portfolio's plus the put's payoffs at time τ equals

$$S_\tau + max[K - S_\tau, 0] = \begin{cases} S_\tau & \text{if} \quad S_\tau \geq K = S_t \\ K = S_t & \text{if} \quad S_\tau < K = S_t \end{cases}$$

The cost of the portfolio insurance is the price of the put option.

13.1.2   Floating Rate Loans

Caps can be used to reduce the risk of a floating rate loan.

Consider a floating rate bond with maturity τ, face value 1 dollar, and paying the default-free spot rate $r(t)$ at times $t = 1, \ldots, T$.

A *cap* with maturity τ and strike k is a portfolio of caplets with the same strike price, unit notional value, and maturities $t = 1, ..., \tau$. Going long the cap gives a payment equal to $max[r(t-1) - k, 0]$ at time t.

The payoff to a cap when summed with the interest paid on the floating rate loan reduces the combined position's payoff to a maximum of k dollars at any payment date.

To see this note that the time t payoff to a floating rate loan plus a cap equals

$$-r(t-1) + max[r(t-1) - k, 0] = \begin{cases} -r(t-1) & \text{if} \quad r(t-1) \leq k \\ -k & \text{if} \quad r(t-1) > k \end{cases}.$$

The cost of this payment insurance is the price of the cap.

13.2   Cost of Carry

This section shows how to synthetically construct a forward contract synthetically using the risky asset and zero-coupon bonds.

Consider a risky asset with time t price S_t. Suppose that the asset has no cash flows over $[0, \tau]$.

Consider a forward contract on this asset with delivery date τ and forward price $K(0, \tau)$. The payoff to the forward contract at the delivery date τ is

$$[S_\tau - K(0, \tau)].$$

To synthetically construct this forward contract's payoffs, buy the underlying risky asset at time 0 and short $K(0, \tau)$ default-free zero-coupon bonds maturing at time τ. The payoff to this portfolio at time τ is

$$[S_\tau - K(0, \tau)].$$

This implies, to avoid arbitrage, that the cost of constructing this portfolio at time 0 must be zero (because the cost of entering a forward contract is zero). Hence,

$$S_t - K(0,\tau)P(0,\tau) = 0 \quad \text{or} \quad K(0,\tau) = \frac{S_t}{P(0,\tau)}.$$

This is the arbitrage-free forward price.

For its use in risk management, one needs to note that this synthetic construction implies that the

$$\text{risky asset} = \text{forward} + \text{buying zeros}.$$

Hence, to remove the asset's price risk from a forward, one can short the risky asset (moving the risky asset from the left side to the right side of the equation).

13.3 Put Call Parity

This section shows how to synthetically construct a European call option using a European put option, the underlying asset, and a zero-coupon bond.

Consider a risky asset with time t price S_t. Suppose that the asset has no cash flows over $[0, \tau]$.

Consider a European call on this asset with maturity date τ and strike price K. The payoff to the call option is

$$max\,[S_\tau - K, 0]\,.$$

To synthetically construct this call option's payoffs, buy a European put on this asset with maturity date τ and strike price K, buy the underlying asset, and short K zero-coupon bonds with maturity τ. The payoff to this portfolio at time τ is:

$$max\,[K - S_\tau, 0] + S_\tau - K = max\,[S_\tau - K, 0]\,.$$

This implies, to avoid arbitrage, that the cost of constructing this portfolio at time 0 must be the value of the European call option. Hence, letting C_0 be the time 0 value of the European call option and $\mathcal{P}_0$ be the time 0 value of the European put option, we have

$$\mathcal{P}_0 + S_0 - KP(0,\tau) = C_0.$$

This is known as put call parity.

For its use in risk management, one needs to note that the synthetic construction implies that the

$$\text{call} = \text{put} + \text{buying asset} + \text{shorting zeros}.$$

Hence, to remove the asset's price risk from a call, one can short both the put and the risky asset (moving them from the right side to the left side of the equation).

13.4 Coupon Bonds

This section shows how to synthetically construct a default-free coupon bond using a basket of default-free zero-coupon bonds. For risky bonds, we also show how to synthetically construct a risky coupon bond using a default-free coupon bond and a CDS.

13.4.1 Default-free

A default-free coupon bond can be synthetically constructed as a portfolio of default-free zeros.

Consider a default-free coupon bond with coupon rate c, maturity date τ, and a face value 1 dollar. Its time t price is denoted $\mathfrak{B}(t, \tau)$ for $0 \leq t \leq \tau \leq T$. The coupon payments occur at times $t = 1, \cdots, \tau$.

The coupon bond's payoffs can be synthetically constructed by the following portfolio of default-free zero-coupon bonds: (i) buy c zero-coupon bonds maturing at times $t = 1, \cdots, \tau$, and (ii) buy 1 extra zero-coupon bond maturing at time τ.

No arbitrage implies

$$\mathfrak{B}(t, \tau) = \sum_{i=t+1}^{\tau-1} cP(t, i) + (c+1)P(t, \tau).$$

This formula for a default-free coupon bond is often used to estimate the prices of the underlying zero-coupon bonds (see Jarrow and Chatterjea [37], Chapter 21).

CDS and a Default-free Bond

Here we show how to synthetically construct a default-free coupon bond via buying a risky coupon bond and buying a CDS with maturity and notional equal to that of the risky coupon bond.

Consider both a risky and default-free coupon bond issued at time 0 with the same maturity τ.

The default-free coupon bond has a coupon rate c, maturity date τ, and face value 1 dollar. Its time t price is denoted $\mathfrak{B}(t,\tau)$ for $0 \le t \le \tau \le T$. The coupon payments occur at times $t = 1, \cdots, \tau$.

The risky coupon bond has a coupon rate c_R, maturity date τ, and face value 1 dollar. Its time t price is denoted $\mathfrak{D}(t,\tau)$ for $0 \le t \le \tau \le T$. The coupon payments also occur at times $t = 1, \cdots, \tau$.

The CDS has a maturity date of τ and a notional of 1 dollar. It pays the rate s per period at times $t = 1, \cdots, \tau$ if no default, and in the event of default at time $\chi \le \tau$, it makes its last payment of s, it receives $\mathfrak{B}(\chi,\tau)$, and it gives up $\mathfrak{D}(\chi,\tau)$.

Note that if $\chi = \tau$, then the CDS receives $\mathfrak{B}(\chi,\tau) = \mathfrak{B}(\tau,\tau) = 1$. If $\chi > \tau$, then the CDS's payoffs are identically 0 because it no longer exists.

In reality the CDS receives the face value of the risky bond at χ, which is 1. In practice, this difference will make the subsequent construction only approximate.

The CDS plus the risky coupon bond payoffs are:

time	0	1	$\cdots$	$\chi - 1$	χ	$\cdots$	τ
CDS		$-s$		$-s$	$-s + \mathfrak{B}(\chi,\tau) - \mathfrak{D}(\chi,\tau)$	0	0
Risky bond		c_R		c_R	$c_R + \mathfrak{D}(\chi,\tau)$	0	0
Sum		$c_R - s$		$c_R - s$	$c_R - s + \mathfrak{B}(\chi,\tau)$	0	0

A default-free coupon bond payoffs given that it is sold at time χ are:

time	0	1	$\cdots$	$\chi - 1$	χ	$\cdots$	τ
Default $-$ free bond		c		c	$c + \mathfrak{B}(\chi,\tau)$	0	0

Note that both payoffs are equivalent in terms of their risks. Hence, the CDS plus a risky coupon bond is equivalent to a default-free coupon bond.

Let C_0 denote the value of the CDS at time 0. Recall that the CDS rate s is that rate which sets $C_0 = 0$.

No arbitrage then implies that

$$\mathfrak{B}(0,\tau) = \mathfrak{D}(0,\tau) + C_0 = \mathfrak{D}(0,\tau).$$

This is true if and only if

$$c_R - s = c \quad \text{or} \quad c_R = c + s.$$

This gives the arbitrage-free relation between the CDS rate and the coupon rates on both the default-free and risky coupon bonds. We see that the CDS spread equals the credit spread on the risky bond above the riskless bond, i.e. $s = c_R - c$.

13.4.2 Risky

To synthetically construct a risky coupon bond, one can buy a default-free zero-coupon bond and sell the CDS. For the construction, see the previous subsection.

13.5 Inverse Floaters

For the purposes of this analysis we assume that the issuer of the inverse floater is default-free. Recall from Chapter 2 that an inverse floater has a maturity date τ, a notional of 1 dollar (without loss of generality), and a coupon rate of c. Its coupon payments are reduced as an underlying floating rate increases (this is the inverse floating aspect).

Let r_t denote the default-free spot rate of interest.

The inverse floater is defined by the following cash flows.

time	0	1	2	...	τ
inverse floater		$max[c - r_0, 0]$	$max[c - r_1, 0]$	...	$max[c - r_{\tau-1}, 0] + 1$

Consider forming a portfolio consisting of: (i) long an ordinary coupon bond with maturity date τ, a notional of 1 dollar, and a coupon rate of c, (ii) short a floating rate bond with maturity date τ and a notional of 1 dollar (here, the floating rate is the default-free spot rate), (iii) long an interest rate cap with maturity date τ and strike price c, and (iv) long a zero-coupon bond maturity at time τ. The payoffs to this portfolio are:

time	0	1	2	...	τ
coupon bond		c	c		$c + 1$
floating rate bond		$-r_0$	$-r_1$		$-r_{\tau-1} - 1$
cap		$max[r_0 - c, 0]$	$max[r_1 - c, 0]$	...	$max[r_{\tau-1} - c, 0]$
zero coupon bond					1
Sum		$max[c - r_0, 0]$	$max[c - r_1, 0]$		$max[c - r_{\tau-1}, 0] + 1$

Since these are the same as the inverse floater's cash flows, no arbitrage implies that

$$\mathfrak{C}_0 = \mathfrak{B}(0, \tau) - 1 + Cap_0 + P(0, \tau)$$

where $\mathfrak{C}_0$ is the time 0 value of the inverse floater, $\mathfrak{B}(0, \tau)$ is the time 0 value of the coupon bond, the floating rate bond is always valued at par (1 dollar), Cap_0 is the time 0 value of the cap, and $P(0, \tau)$ is the time 0 value of a zero-coupon bond with maturity τ.

13.6   Interest Rate Swaps

This section shows how to synthetically construct an interest rate swap from a portfolio of FRAs and zero-coupon bonds.

Consider a (plain vanilla) paying fixed, receiving floating interest rate swap with swap rate c, a maturity date τ, and a notional of 1 dollar.

The swap's payoffs are:

time	0	1	$\cdots$	t	$\cdots$	τ
Swap		$[r_0 - c]$		$[r_{t-1} - c]$		$[r_{\tau-1} - c]$

Next, construct a portfolio consisting of one FRA maturing at times $t = 1, \cdots, \tau$ with FRA rates $a_1, \cdots, a_\tau$ and buying $(a_t - c)$ default-free zero-coupon bonds maturing at times $t = 1, \cdots, \tau$. The payoffs to this portfolio are:

time	0	1	$\cdots$	t	$\cdots$	τ
FRAs		$[r_0 - a_1]$		$[r_{t-1} - a_t]$		$[r_{\tau-1} - a_\tau]$
Zeros		$[a_1 - c]$		$[a_t - c]$		$[a_\tau - c]$
Sum		$[r_0 - c]$		$[r_{t-1} - c]$		$[r_{\tau-1} - c]$

This shows that the portfolio of FRAs and zero-coupon bonds exactly match the payoffs to the swap, proving the stated result.

For its use in risk management, one needs to note that this synthetic construction implies that the

$$\text{swap} = \text{portfolio FRAs} + \text{portfolio zeros}.$$

Hence, to remove the interest rate risk from a swap for any intermediate time period, one can short the relevant FRA and zero (moving them from the right side to the left side of the equation).

Chapter 14

Dynamic Hedging

Under a complete market, dynamic hedging enables one to synthetically construct any derivative. The ability to synthetically construct implies the ability to remove all risks. When markets are incomplete, synthetic construction is usually impossible. In this case, dynamic hedging only enables one to super- and sub-replicate the payoffs to any derivative. To use dynamic hedging we need to assume an evolution for the underlying traded assets. For simplicity of the presentation, we assume that there is no interest rate risk and restrict ourselves to the market in Chapter 3. The subsequent analysis can easily be extended to include interest rate risk using the HJM model in Chapter 4. The same methodology presented below applies, but in an extended fashion with more complex notation.

14.1 Set up

This set up is from Chapter 3. We consider a continuous time and finite horizon $[0, T]$ model. The uncertainty is captured by a filtered probability space satisfying the usual conditions $(\Omega, \mathcal{F}, (\mathcal{F}_t), \mathbb{P})$. The random state of the economy over $[0, T]$ is an element $\omega \in \Omega$. The information flows over time are captured by the filtration $(\mathcal{F}_t)$. And, the likelihood of the states is given by the statistical probability (measure) $\mathbb{P}$.

As before, we impose the following assumptions.

Frictionless and competitive markets.

Frictionless means that there are no transactions costs and no trading constraints, e.g. short sale constraints or margin requirements. Competitive means that all traders act as price takers, believing that there trades have no quantity impact on the price.

No interest rate risk.

Traded is a money market account with initial value $B_0 = 1$ and time $t \in [0, T]$ value

$$B_t = e^{rt} \tag{14.1}$$

where r, the default-free spot rate of interest, is a constant.

Risky asset price evolution.

Traded is a risky asset whose market price at time $t \in [0, T]$ is denoted by S_t. We assume that $S > 0$, that the risky asset has no cash flows, and that

$$S_t = S_0 + \int_0^t \mu_S(u)du + \int_0^t \sigma_S(u)dL(u)$$

where $L(t)$ is a Brownian motion under $\mathbb{P}$, capturing the randomness in the evolution of the asset price process with $L(0) = 0$, and μ_S, σ_S are very general stochastic processes, depending upon the state of the economy.

Over a small time interval $[t, t + \triangle t]$ this evolution can be approximated by

$$\triangle S_t = \mu_S(t)\triangle t + \sigma_S(t)\triangle L(t) \tag{14.2}$$

where $\triangle S_t = S_{t+\triangle t} - S_t$ and $\triangle L(t) = L(t + \triangle t) - L(t)$.

To facilitate the subsequent analysis, we assume that S_t is a Markov process (see Protter [56] for a definition).

We assume that the evolution is such that it satisfies both NFLVR (no arbitrage) and ND (no dominance). By the third fundamental theorem of asset pricing this implies that there exists a risk-neutral probability $\mathbb{Q}$ such that

$$S_t = E^{\mathbb{Q}}\left(\frac{S_T}{B_T} | \mathcal{F}_t\right) B_t \qquad \text{for all } t.$$

Hence, under this structure there are no asset price bubbles. The market can be complete or incomplete. We study both cases below.

14.2   Complete Markets

In this section, we assume that the filtration $\mathcal{F}_t$ in the underlying filtered probability space is the filtration generated by the Brownian motion $L(t)$.

This implies that there is only one source of uncertainty in the asset price process.

Assuming that $\sigma_S(t) > 0$ for all t with probability one, this implies that the market is complete.

Given the Markov process assumption imposed above, this implies that the drift and volatility can be written as deterministic functions of t, S_t, i.e. $\mu_S(t) = g_1(t, S_t)$ and $\sigma_S(t) = g_2(t, S_t)$ where $g_i(\cdot, \cdot)$ for $i = 1, 2$ are deterministic functions.

This observation shows that the volatility can be stochastic. This class of asset price models are sometimes called *local volatility* models.

Next, let us consider an arbitrary derivative $C_T \in \mathcal{L}_+^0$ with $E^{\mathbb{Q}}\left(\frac{C_T}{B_T}\right) < \infty$. Since the market is complete, by the second fundamental theorem of asset pricing, we can use risk-neutral valuation to price the derivative:

$$C_t = E^{\mathbb{Q}}\left(\frac{C_T}{B_T}\,|\mathcal{F}_t\right) B_t \qquad \text{for all } t.$$

Again, under the Markov assumption we can rewrite the derivative's value as a deterministic function of t, S_t, i.e. $C_t = f(t, S_t)$ where $f(\cdot, \cdot)$ is a deterministic function. To simplify the notation in the subsequent analysis we write

$$C_t = C(t, S_t). \tag{14.3}$$

This double use of C should cause no confusion. We note that suppressed in this functional representation is the default-free spot rate r, which is a constant parameter in the model.

14.2.1 Taylor Series Expansion

The basic approach to dynamic hedging is to use a Taylor series expansion over $[t, t + \triangle]$ on C_t in conjunction with static hedging to remove all of the risk in a derivative position. The hedging instruments can be the underlying assets or other derivatives. There are two cases to study, depending upon the size of the time interval $\triangle$: large and small.

Large $\triangle$: *($(\triangle S_t)^2$ is random)*

Assuming that $C(t, S_t)$ is appropriately differentiable, we can apply a Taylor series expansion to get

$$\triangle C_t = \frac{\partial C}{\partial t}\triangle + \frac{\partial C}{\partial S_t}\triangle S_t + \frac{1}{2}\frac{\partial^2 C}{\partial S_t^2}(\triangle S_t)^2 + \varepsilon(\triangle S_t) \tag{14.4}$$

where $\triangle C_t = C_{t+\triangle} - C_t$, $\triangle S_t = S_{t+\triangle} - S_t$, and $\varepsilon(\triangle S_t)$ is the error in the approximation.

It can be shown that the error in the approximation, $\varepsilon(\triangle S_t)$, is small relative to the remaining terms and can be ignored (see Rudin [57], p. 110).

Small $\triangle$: *($(\triangle S_t)^2$ is approximately deterministic)*

If $\triangle$ is small, we have:

$$(\triangle S_t)^2 = (\mu_S(t)\triangle t + \sigma_t \triangle L(t))^2$$
$$= \sigma_t^2 \triangle. \tag{14.5}$$

In the limit as $\triangle \to 0$, this implies that $(\triangle S_t)^2$ is deterministic. Substituting this into expression (14.4) yields:

$$\triangle C_t = \frac{\partial C}{\partial t}\triangle + \frac{\partial C}{\partial S_t}\triangle S_t + \frac{1}{2}\frac{\partial^2 C}{\partial S_t^2}\sigma_t^2\triangle + \varepsilon(\triangle S_t). \tag{14.6}$$

Note that the error in the approximation, $\varepsilon(\triangle S_t)$, is small and ignored. Expression (14.5) gives the meaning of the phrase "small." It implies that for small enough $\triangle$, the random quantity $(\triangle S_t)^2$ is deterministic. This follows from the properties of the quadratic variation of a stochastic process (see Protter [56] for a definition of the quadratic variation and a formal statement of this result).

Hence, over a small time period $\triangle$, $(\triangle S)^2$ is non-random and "locally" riskless. This implies that the randomness in the change in the derivative's value over $[t, t + \triangle]$ is proportional to (a linear function of) the change in the underlying asset price process.

14.2.2 Delta $\left(\frac{\partial C}{\partial S}\right)$ Hedging

Suppose that we have a long position in the derivative C_t and we want to remove all of the asset's price risk from this position over the time period $[t, t + \triangle]$. Why? Perhaps the derivative was undervalued when purchased, and we want to lock in the arbitrage profits.

Let us assume that $\triangle$ is small, hence $(\triangle S)^2$ is non-random.

To create the riskless position, we start by forming a portfolio consisting of the derivative and shorting n shares of the risky asset. The time t value of this portfolio is:

$$V_t = C_t - nS_t.$$

Next, we want to choose n so that

$$var(\triangle V_t) = var(\triangle C_t - n\triangle S_t) = 0$$

where $var(\cdot)$ denotes variance.

Substitution of expression (14.6) yields

$$var\left(\triangle V_t\right) = var\left(\frac{\partial C}{\partial t}\triangle + \frac{\partial C}{\partial S_t}\triangle S_t + \frac{1}{2}\frac{\partial^2 C}{\partial S_t^2}\sigma_t^2\triangle - n\triangle S_t\right)$$

$$= \left[\frac{\partial C}{\partial S_t} - n\right]^2 var\left(\triangle S_t\right).$$

This variance will be zero if and only if

$$n = \frac{\partial C}{\partial S_t}.$$

This procedure is called *delta hedging* because n is the derivative's *delta*. Note that shorting n shares of the risky asset will remove all of the price risk from a long position in the derivative over a small time period $\triangle$.

This portfolio will be riskless over $[t, t + \triangle]$. Hence, there exists an $m \in \mathbb{R}$ such that $V_t = mB_t$, i.e. the portfolio is equivalent to an investment in the money market account. This implies that the synthetic derivative position can be written as

$$X_t = mB_t + nS_t$$

where $m = \frac{V_t}{B_t} = \frac{C_t - nS_t}{B_t}$.

To maintain this riskless position across time, the portfolio will need to be rebalanced at time $t + \triangle$. In theory (in the continuous time limit), this rebalancing will be self-financing requiring no cash inflow or outflow. For discrete hedging, however, to rebalance the hedged position some small additional cash inflow/outflow may be required.

Although this argument shows how to remove all the risk from holding the derivative, it is obvious that if one shorts a fraction of n shares, then only a fraction of the asset price risk will be removed over the time interval $[t, t + \triangle]$.

14.2.3 Gamma $\left(\frac{\partial^2 C}{\partial S^2}\right)$ Hedging

In theory one can trade continuously, so that $\triangle$ can be made arbitrarily small. In practice, however, one cannot trade continuously. If $\triangle$ is small enough, then $(\triangle S)^2$ is approximately non-random. However, if $\triangle$ is too large, then $(\triangle S)^2$ is random and this component needs to be hedged as well. When $\triangle$ is large, there are two risks: $(\triangle S, (\triangle S)^2)$. To understand why they are different risks, note that these risks behave differently since $S_t \lessgtr 0$, but $S_t^2 > 0$. To hedge these two risks $(\triangle S, (\triangle S)^2)$, we need an additional risky asset to add to the portfolio. Let's choose another derivative $D_T \in \mathcal{L}_+^0$ with $E^{\mathbb{Q}}\left(\frac{D_T}{B_T}\right) < \infty$ on the underlying risky asset S_t.

To create the riskless portfolio, we start by forming a portfolio consisting of the derivative C_t, short n shares of the risky asset, and short m shares of the derivative D_t. The time t value of this portfolio is:

$$V_t = C_t - nS_t - mD_t.$$

Next, we want to choose n, m so that

$$var\left(\triangle V_t\right) = var\left(\triangle C_t - n\triangle S_t - m\triangle D_t\right) = 0.$$

Substitution of expression (14.4) for C_t and D_t yields:

$$var\left(\triangle V_t\right) = var\left(\frac{\partial C}{\partial t}\triangle + \frac{\partial C}{\partial S_t}\triangle S_t + \frac{1}{2}\frac{\partial^2 C}{\partial S_t^2}\left(\triangle S_t\right)^2 - n\triangle S_t \right.$$
$$\left. -m\frac{\partial D}{\partial t}\triangle - m\frac{\partial D}{\partial S_t}\triangle S_t - m\frac{1}{2}\frac{\partial^2 D}{\partial S_t^2}\left(\triangle S_t\right)^2\right)$$
$$= var\left(\left[\frac{\partial C}{\partial S_t} - n - m\frac{\partial D}{\partial S_t}\right]\triangle S_t + \frac{1}{2}\left[\frac{\partial^2 C}{\partial S_t^2} - m\frac{\partial^2 D}{\partial S_t^2}\right]\left(\triangle S_t\right)^2\right) = 0.$$

This will be zero if

$$\frac{\partial C}{\partial S_t} - n - m\frac{\partial D}{\partial S_t} = 0 \quad \text{and}$$
$$\frac{\partial^2 C}{\partial S_t^2} - m\frac{\partial^2 D}{\partial S_t^2} = 0.$$

The solution is

$$n = \frac{\partial C}{\partial S_t} - \frac{\frac{\partial^2 C}{\partial S_t^2}}{\frac{\partial^2 D}{\partial S_t^2}}\frac{\partial D}{\partial S_t} \quad \text{and} \quad m = \frac{\frac{\partial^2 C}{\partial S_t^2}}{\frac{\partial^2 D}{\partial S_t^2}}.$$

This is called *gamma hedging* because $\left(\frac{\partial^2 C}{\partial S^2}\right)$ is the derivative's gamma. We note that to maintain this riskless position across time t, the portfolio will need to be rebalanced at time $t + \triangle$. Because $\triangle$ is large, this rebalancing will not be self-financing and it may require a small cash inflow or outflow.

Although this argument shows how to remove all of the risk from holding the derivative, it is obvious that if one shorts a fraction of n, m shares, then only a fraction of the asset price risk will be removed.

14.2.4   Vega ($\frac{\partial C}{\partial \sigma}$) Hedging

Vega hedging describes removing volatility risk from a derivative portfolio. There are two cases to study: local volatility models and stochastic volatility models.

Local Volatility: $(\sigma_S(t) = g(t, S_t)$ *for* $g(\cdot, \cdot)$ *a deterministic function)*

This is the model studied above. In this model, volatility is not stochastic at time t since S_t is known at time t, but it is stochastic at time $t + \Delta$. Hence, delta hedging is sufficient to remove all of the asset's price risk from a derivative portfolio over $[t, t+\Delta]$ because there is no volatility risk "locally at time t."

Example. *(Vega Hedging in the Black Scholes and Libor Models)*

Special cases of this observation are the Black-Scholes formula for pricing call options and the Libor model for pricing caplets (see Jarrow and Chatterjea [37], Chapters 19 and 25). These models assume that the volatility of the underlying asset is a constant. Hence, there is no volatility risk in these models. Unfortunately, however, volatilities are stochastic in practice. Consequently, delta hedging the asset price risk alone does not create a riskless position. When these models are used, adhoc procedures are often employed in an attempt to remove the volatility risk. We describe this adhoc procedure now.

In the Black-Scholes or Libor model, $\sigma_S(t) = \sigma > 0$ where σ is a constant. In this case, first write the derivative's value as $C_t = C(t, S_t, \sigma)$. Second, perform a Taylor series expansion around $(t, \Delta S_t, \Delta\sigma)$. Last, hedge changes in $(t, \Delta S_t, \Delta\sigma)$ over a small time period Δ by choosing the shares in the underlying stock and another distinct derivative so that the change in the portfolio's value, after substitution of the first order Taylor series expansion, has zero variance. This mathematics is analogous to that used in gamma hedging.

Unfortunately, since $\Delta\sigma = 0$, this Taylor series expansion gives nonsensical results. This adhoc vega hedging does not work. Indeed, how can the model tell how to hedge volatility risk, when there is no volatility risk in the model? The answer is that it cannot (see Jarrow and Chatterjea [37] for a more detailed argument). This is called *vega hedging* because $\left(\frac{\partial C}{\partial \sigma}\right)$ is called the derivative's vega. This completes the example.

Stochastic Volatility: $(\sigma_S(t) = \sigma_t$ *depends on a second Brownian Motion)*

Volatility risk occurs when $\sigma_S(t)$ depends on the evolution of a second Brownian motion. To understand this situation, assume that the filtration $\mathcal{F}_t$ in the underlying filtered probability space is generated by two independent Brownian motions $L(t), M(t)$. This implies that there are now two sources of uncertainty in the asset price process.

As before, the stock price process satisfies expression (14.2), and we assume the volatility $\sigma_S(t) \equiv \sigma_t$ is stochastic and satisfies the following evolution:

$$\sigma_t = \sigma_0 + \int_0^t \eta(u, S_u, \sigma_u)du + \int_0^t v(u, S_u, \sigma_u)dM(u)$$

where $\eta(\cdot), v(\cdot)$ are suitably integrable, deterministic functions of the arguments.

Over the time interval $[t, t + \Delta]$, this evolution can be approximated by

$$\triangle\sigma_t = \eta(t, S_t, \sigma_t)\triangle t + v(t, S_t, \sigma_t)\triangle M(t) \qquad (14.7)$$

where $\triangle\sigma_t = \sigma_{t+\triangle} - \sigma_t$ and $\triangle M(t) = M(t + \triangle) - M(t)$. We assume that this evolution is a Markov process.

We assume that the market is complete. For this to be the case we need trading in another risky asset subject to these same two risks. This asset is usually a derivative on the risky asset, e.g. a call or put option.

Next, let us consider an arbitrary derivative $C_T \in \mathcal{L}_+^0$ with $E^{\mathbb{Q}}\left(\frac{C_T}{B_T}\right) < \infty$. Following the same logic as that used above, the derivative's arbitrage-free value can be written as:

$$C_t = C(t, S_t, \sigma_t) \qquad (14.8)$$

where $C(\cdot)$ is a deterministic function of its arguments. Assuming that $C(\cdot)$ is appropriately differentiable, we can a apply Taylor series expansion to obtain

$$\triangle C_t = \frac{\partial C}{\partial t}\triangle + \frac{\partial C}{\partial S_t}\triangle S_t + \frac{1}{2}\frac{\partial^2 C}{\partial S_t^2}(\triangle S_t)^2$$
$$+ \frac{\partial C}{\partial \sigma_t}\triangle\sigma_t + \frac{1}{2}\frac{\partial^2 C}{\partial \sigma_t^2}(\triangle\sigma_t)^2 + \frac{\partial^2 C}{\partial S_t\partial\sigma_t}\triangle S_t\triangle\sigma_t + \varepsilon(\triangle S_t).$$

Over a small time interval $\triangle$, as before one can show that:

$$(\triangle S_t)^2 = \sigma_t^2\triangle,$$
$$(\triangle\sigma)^2 = v_t^2\triangle, \quad \text{and}$$
$$\triangle S_t\triangle\sigma_t = 0.$$

Substitution yields

$$\triangle C_t = \frac{\partial C}{\partial t}\triangle + \frac{\partial C}{\partial S_t}\triangle S_t + \frac{1}{2}\frac{\partial^2 C}{\partial S_t^2}\sigma_t^2\triangle$$
$$+ \frac{\partial C}{\partial \sigma_t}\triangle\sigma_t + \frac{1}{2}\frac{\partial^2 C}{\partial \sigma_t^2}\sigma_t^2\triangle + \varepsilon(\triangle S_t).$$

To remove both the price and volatility risk from the derivative position, we form a portfolio consisting of the derivative C_t, short n shares of the risky asset, and short m shares of the derivative D_t. The time t value of the portfolio is:

$$V_t = C_t - nS_t - mD_t.$$

We want to choose n, m so that

$$var\left(\triangle V_t\right) = var\left(\triangle C_t - n\triangle S_t - m\triangle D_t\right) = 0.$$

Substitution of the Taylor series expansion yields

$$var\left(\triangle V_t\right) = var\left(\frac{\partial C}{\partial t}\triangle + \frac{\partial C}{\partial S_t}\triangle S_t + \frac{1}{2}\frac{\partial^2 C}{\partial S_t^2}\sigma_t^2\triangle + \frac{\partial C}{\partial \sigma_t}\triangle\sigma_t + \frac{1}{2}\frac{\partial^2 C}{\partial \sigma_t^2}\left(\triangle\sigma_t\right)^2\right.$$
$$\left. -n\triangle S_t - m\frac{\partial D}{\partial t}\triangle - m\frac{\partial D}{\partial S_t}\triangle S_t - \frac{m}{2}\frac{\partial^2 D}{\partial S_t^2}v_t^2\triangle - m\frac{\partial D}{\partial \sigma_t}\triangle\sigma_t - \frac{m}{2}\frac{\partial^2 D}{\partial \sigma_t^2}\left(\triangle\sigma_t\right)^2\right)$$
$$= var\left(\left[\frac{\partial C}{\partial S_t} - n - m\frac{\partial D}{\partial S_t}\right]\triangle S_t + \left[\frac{\partial C}{\partial \sigma_t} - m\frac{\partial D}{\partial \sigma_t}\right]\triangle\sigma_t\right) = 0.$$

This will be zero if

$$\frac{\partial C}{\partial S_t} - n - m\frac{\partial D}{\partial S_t} = 0, \quad \text{and}$$
$$\frac{\partial C}{\partial \sigma_t} - m\frac{\partial D}{\partial \sigma_t} = 0.$$

The solution is

$$n = \frac{\partial C}{\partial S_t} - \frac{\frac{\partial C}{\partial \sigma_t}}{\frac{\partial D}{\partial \sigma_t}}\frac{\partial D}{\partial S_t} \quad \text{and} \quad m = \frac{\frac{\partial C}{\partial \sigma_t}}{\frac{\partial D}{\partial \sigma_t}}.$$

This is valid application of vega hedging because the derivative pricing formula includes volatility risk over the time period $[t, t + \triangle]$ that is independent of the asset price risk.

14.3 Incomplete Markets

In an incomplete market, by definition, one cannot synthetically construct all derivatives' payoffs using a self-financing trading strategy. In this case one can super- and sub-replicate the derivative's payoffs. We have already discussed this in Chapter 6 when studying liquidity risk and in Chapter 8 when studying trading constraints.

Recall from Chapter 3 that a trading strategy is a pair of holdings in the money market account and risky asset $(\alpha_B(t), \alpha_S(t))$ for all t with initial wealth $X_0 = x$ and time t value $X_t = \alpha_B(t)B_t + \alpha_S(t)S_t$. Let $\mathcal{A}(x)$ be the set of all admissible self-financing trading strategies starting with initial wealth x. Let us consider an arbitrary derivative $C_T \in \mathcal{L}_+^0$ with $E^{\mathbb{Q}}\left(\frac{C_T}{B_T}\right) < \infty$ where $\mathbb{Q}$ is a risk-neutral probability. Recall that in this case, the risk-neutral probability $\mathbb{Q}$ is not unique.

14.3.1   Super- and Sub-Replication

Although we cannot exactly synthetically construct the derivative's payoffs, we can obtain upper and lower bounds for these payoffs. The upper and lower bounds for the payoffs imply upper and lower bounds for the price of the derivative security, which if violated generate an arbitrage opportunity.

The upper bound on the derivative's price is defined as follows.

Definition 14.1. Given a derivative C_T, the *super-replication price* is defined by

$$\overline{C}_t = inf\left\{x : \ \exists(\alpha_B(t), \alpha_S(t)) \in \mathcal{A}(x) \ s.t. \ X_T \geq C_T\right\}. \qquad (14.9)$$

The super-replication price corresponds to the smallest amount x that one can invest to sell the derivative and pay off the derivative's liabilities with the proceeds from the investment. In this definition we see the super-replication trading strategy must be determined as the solution to an optimization problem. It is that self-financing trading strategy $(\alpha_B(t), \alpha_S(t))$ that attains the upper bound.

In an analogous fashion, we can obtain the lower bound on the derivative's price.

Definition 14.2. Given a derivative C_T, the *sub-replication price* is defined by

$$\underline{C}_t = sup\left\{x : \ \exists(\alpha_B(t), \alpha_S(t)) \in \mathcal{A}(x) \ s.t. \ X_T \leq C_T\right\}. \qquad (14.10)$$

The sub-replication price corresponds to the largest amount x that one can borrow to buy the derivative and pay off the loan with the proceeds from the derivative. Again, in this definition we see the sub-replication trading strategy must be determined as the solution to an optimization problem. It is that self-financing trading strategy $(\alpha_B(t), \alpha_S(t))$ that attains the lower bound.

14.3.2   Valuation and Hedging

Given these concepts, we get the following result.

Theorem 14.3. *Super- and Sub-Replication Prices*
  Let $\mathbb{Q}$ be any risk-neutral probability (recall it is non-unique).
  Given a derivative C_T with $E^{\mathbb{Q}}\left(\frac{C_T}{B_T}\right) < \infty$, then

$$\overline{C}_t \geq E^{\mathbb{Q}}\left(\frac{C_T}{B_T} | \mathcal{F}_t\right) B_t \geq \underline{C}_t \qquad (14.11)$$

for all t.

The inequality is strict for a derivative C_T whose payoff cannot be written as a linear function of B_T, S_T.

For a proof see Pham [54], chapter 7.

To get exact values for $\overline{C}_t, \underline{C}_t$, one needs to solve the optimization problems given in the definitions of the super- and sub-replication prices. This is a difficult exercise that almost always requires a numerical procedure. More importantly for risk management, the super- and sub- replication strategies $(\alpha_B(t), \alpha_S(t))$ that attain the upper and lower bounds implicit in these prices must be obtained numerically as well. In practice, these procedures are not often employed. Due to the complexity of these computations, static hedging of derivatives using other traded assets and derivatives is used instead.

Part VI

Case Studies

Overview

This part applies the tools and insights obtained from the previous parts to understand famous risk management failures. By understanding these risk management failures, one can gain insights into how to correctly risk manage a balance sheet. The famous risk management failures studied in chronological order are Penn Square Bank 1992, Metallgesellschaft 1993, Orange County 1994, Barings Bank 1995, Long Term Capital Management 1998, the Credit Crisis 2007, and Washington Mutual 2008.

The conclusion from studying these examples can be summarized with the following three simple risk management rules.

1. Understand your returns (includes proper monitoring and accounting procedures).

2. Set up proper incentives.

3. Control funding risk.

Each of these rules will be explained in turn.

Understand Your Returns

The first rule for risk management is to *understand the source of your returns*. The wisdom of this maxim is self-evident for *negative returns*. Thus, the essence of this statement is to *understand the source of your positive returns*.

The violation of this maxim was a cause of the risk management failures in all the subsequent case studies. To understand the source of your returns, the subsequent blueprint should be followed.

1. First, decompose your returns into expected returns and residuals. The *expected returns* can be decomposed, for example using Jarrow and Protter [40], into compensation for systematic risk (betas) and abnormal returns (alpha).

2. By construction, the expected compensation for systematic risk is understood. If there is *model error* in the determination of the systematic risk factors, then failures can occur, e.g. this partially explains the failures of Metallgesellschaft (incorrect hedging) and Long Term Capital Management (incorrect understanding of liquidity risk). This leaves understanding the sources of the abnormal returns.

3. Abnormal returns can be generated in four ways.

    (a) Fraud (from delegated management). If the abnormal return is due to fraud, then failures can occur. This source explains Barings Bank's failure, and it partially explains Penn Square Bank's and Washington Mutual's failures.

    (b) Arbitrage opportunities. If the abnormal return is due to an arbitrage opportunity, then the reason for the existence of the trading strategy needs to be identified to verify its validity. For example, in the credit crisis, the misratings of structured debt by credit rating agencies led to the existence of rating arbitrage. For Barings Bank, alleged arbitrage opportunities were fraudulently fabricated via accounting manipulation.

    (c) Asset Price Bubbles. If the abnormal return is due to an asset price bubble, one must recognize that the bubble will eventually burst. If the negative returns due to the bubble bursting are unacceptable, then the trading strategy can be hedged by buying or synthetically constructing "insurance," e.g. buying a put option. Benefiting from asset price bubbles and not understanding its consequences when bursting partially explains the failures of Penn Square Bank and Washington Mutual.

    (d) Selling (synthetic) Put Options. If the abnormal returns are due to omitted risks, then the trading strategy effectively is equivalent to selling put options. That is, premiums are received for the insurance, but if the risk events occur, large losses are possible. Not understanding omitted risks partially explains Orange County's failure.

Set up Proper Incentives

Incentives should be based on deviations from expected returns. Expected returns are determined in Rule 1. Improper incentives were a root cause of the risk management failures in all the subsequent case studies.

1. Expected returns set "normal" compensation. This includes compensation for systematic risk and abnormal returns. Deviations from expected returns should determine the "incentive" compensation.

2. Deviations due to random luck (good or bad) should be ignored.

3. Positive deviations due to management actions should be rewarded.

Improper incentives and monitoring were a key cause in all of the subsequent risk management failures.

Control Funding Risk

An entity's leverage in conjunction with its investments determines the balance sheet's risk (standard deviations, correlations). Funding risk was a key element in the risk management failures for all of the subsequent case studies.

A balance sheet without leverage cannot default, it can only become insolvent. A balance sheet with leverage can default. Default incurs financial distress costs and often leads to insolvency. Default is affected by funding risk, which is the conjunction of liquidity risk and binding borrowing constraints. The inability to sell assets quickly at favorable prices without a large quantity impact from trading is the liquidity risk component. The need to liquidate can occur in a "bank run," due to the removal of short term borrowing (e.g. withdrawal of deposits (banks), collateral or margin calls) by creditors when the fear of default becomes large. This is the binding borrowing constraint.

Funding risk contingency planning (e.g. lines of credit, keeping the leverage ratio small) can reduce this risk, and therefore, the probability of default. A balance sheet should set its leverage to a meet a predetermined (acceptable) probability of default. Conceptually, the probability of default should be determined as an implication of an entity's global risk management solution. This probability can be estimated using standard procedures (see Chapter 5).

Chapter 15

Penn Square Bank (1982)

The references for this Chapter are Zweig [58] and the FDIC [19].

15.1 Summary

Penn Square Bank was a small bank located in a shopping mall in Oklahoma City, Oklahoma. Oklahoma's state banking laws allowed a bank to have only one branch[1]. Penn Square Bank was the wholly owned subsidiary of a bank holding company Penn Square[2]. Bank holding companies are allowed more flexibility in their activities than are ordinary banks (Zweig [58], p. 27). In 1980 Penn Square Bank had assets totaling $229 million dollars[3].

Over the period 1976 - 1982, Penn Square Bank invested in and originated an enormous quantity of oil and gas mortgage loans that were participated in by (or sold to) larger banks including the Continental Illinois National Bank and Trust Company (Zweig [58], p. 68), the Seattle First National Bank, Chicago's Northern Trust Company[4], the Michigan National Bank of Lansing[5], Chase Manhattan Bank[6] and 47 other banks around the U.S.[7]. Between October 1981 and June 1982 Penn Square Bank originated $1.3 billion dollars in these energy loans[8]. These oil and gas mortgage loans were very risky and not properly documented[9].

---

[1] Zweig [58], p. 12
[2] Zweig [58], p. 29
[3] Zweig [58], p. 174
[4] Zweig [58], Chapter 10
[5] Zweig [58], p. 149
[6] Zweig [58], p. 168
[7] Zweig [58], p. 249
[8] Zweig [58], p. 240
[9] Zweig [58], Chapter 12

The beginning of Penn Square Bank's trading strategy can be traced to the purchase of the bank by Bill Jennings in mid-December 1975[10]. In the late 70's and early 80's, the U.S. economy was in the midst of a deep recession, interest rates were high and volatile, and inflation was rampant[11]. The recession was partly attributable to an increase in oil prices due to energy shortages caused by political turmoil in the middle East[12]. In the midst of this period (November of 1979), deep-well natural gas prices were deregulated spurring an increase in deep-well natural gas prices. Non-deep well natural gas prices were regulated and capped.

The U.S. energy shortages created a market climate where excessive and imprudent lending and origination of loans by Penn Square Bank to poor credits with inadequate collateral helped to create a price bubble in oil and gas partnership equity shares[13] and oil and gas leases[14].

To fund its loan portfolio, Penn Square Bank sold jumbo certificate of deposits (CDs) at above market rates[15]. Jumbo CDs are in notionals of greater than $100 thousand. In 1981 it funding via CDs was $100 million[16]. Penn Square also sold bank stock (to increase its capital base and fund its loan portfolio) in 1981 to its existing borrowers (customers) by providing them additional loans (based on their original collateral) for the purposes of buying Penn Square Bank stock[17].

The high prices for energy eventually reduced the demand for energy usage. As the demand declined, prices followed. Oil prices started to decline in April 1981[18]. Oil and gas partnership equity shares and lease prices reached their peak in the fall of 1981[19] and declined thereafter. By March and April of 1982, numerous oil and gas mortgage loans on Penn Square Bank's books exhibited non-payment problems that could not be resolved. An Office of the Controller of the Currency (OCC)'s examination of the bank in May/June 1982 revealed that the bank had enormous unrecognized loan losses, had violated numerous banking regulations including exceeding the lending limit on various loans, and was most likely insolvent[20].

The bank officially failed and was taken over by the Federal Deposit Insurance Corporation (FDIC) on July 5, 1982. At the time of its failure, Penn Square's deposits totaled $407.4 million, with approximately $207.5

---

[10]Zweig [58], p. 29
[11]Zweig [58], p. 107
[12]Zweig [58], p. 93
[13]Zweig [58], Chapter 12
[14]Zweig [58], p. 158
[15]Zweig [58], p. 128, 223
[16]Zweig [58], p. 219
[17]Zweig [58], p. 226
[18]Zweig [58], p. 175, 192
[19]Zweig [58], p. 214, 266
[20]Zweig [58], Chapters 30, 33, 35

million insured. The deposits were held by individuals and small businesses, 44 S&L Associations, 29 commercial banks, and 221 credit unions. Penn Square had $516.8 million in assets (FDIC [19], p. 527), it sold over $2 billion in loan participations, and issued almost $1 billion in letters of credit (FDIC [19], p. 540).

Penn Square Bank's losses to uninsured deposits (greater than $100 thousand) and participating banks totaled at least $1.3 billion dollars. On the uninsured deposits, it paid $.55 per dollar deposit (a 45% loss rate) (FDIC [19], p. 538). Penn Square's activities lead to the failure or financial distress of the following banks: Abilene National, First National Bank of Midland, United American Bank of Knoxville, Seattle First, and Continental Illinois[21].

15.2   The Trading Strategy

This section describes the trading strategy in a simplified fashion to highlight the economics involved. Penn Square Bank invested primarily (80% in 1981[22]) in a portfolio of oil and gas related loans including *oil and gas mortgage loans* and loans related to drilling rigs[23]. The oil and gas mortgage loans were issued to *oil and gas partnerships*. Both of these entities are defined below.

The trading strategy speculated on the performance of these energy loans. Penn Square Bank's portfolio consisted of highly concentrated risk in these oil and gas mortgage loans. Via these loans, Penn Square Bank speculated on deep-well natural gas prices (wells deeper than 15,000 feet). Deep natural gas wells were the primary collateral underlying the majority of Penn Square Bank's mortgage loans. As noted earlier, deep-well natural gas could be sold at deregulated prices due to the November 1, 1979 Natural Gas Policy Act[24], in contrast to non-deep-well natural gas prices which were regulated with capped prices.

15.2.1   Oil and Gas Partnerships

An oil and gas partnership is a limited liability company with the following balance sheet.

---

[21] Zweig [58], p. 419
[22] Zweig [58], p. 216
[23] Zweig [58], p. 193
[24] Zweig [58], p. 107

Assets	Liabilities
oil and gas leases (reserves under ground)	mortgage loans
drilling equipment including rigs	
letters of credit	Equity

Oil and Gas Leases

Oil and gas leases are financial contracts that give the owner of the lease the right to drill for oil or gas on someone else's property. The contract has a maturity (say 10 years). If the drilling is not done by the maturity of the lease, the lease expires. If drilling takes place, the owner of the property gets a percentage of the revenues generated by the drilling. The owner of the lease gets the remaining percentage of the revenues. The owner of the lease bears all the costs of the drilling. To grant the lease, the owner of the property usually gets an upfront fee.

Letters of Credit

A *letter of credit* is an American type option issued by a bank with a maturity date τ and strike price $K = 0$, where the underlying is (the right to borrow using) a fixed (or floating) rate loan from the bank with a notional of N dollars for a fixed coupon rate i (or floating rate i_t) for T years. Note that the strike price of the option is 0 dollars. To obtain a letter of credit, the long must pay the option's premium, usually 1 to 2 percent of the notional amount of the underlying loan.

15.2.2   Oil and Gas Mortgage Loans

An *oil and gas mortgage loan* is a fixed rate (floating rate) loan where the underlying collateral for the loan consists of oil and gas leases. The loan has a notional of N dollars, a maturity date T (say 5 years), and a fixed (floating) interest rate i (1 or 2% above prime). If a fixed rate loan, it is often a balloon loan, i.e. the interest is paid at maturity[25]. There are mortgage origination fees paid by the borrower.

Banks are restricted by regulators (banking laws) to the maximum amount they can lend to a single borrower as a percentage of the bank's equity capital (for Penn Square Bank this was $400,000[26]). Due to Penn State's lending constraint, for large oil and gas mortgage loans, two banks participated in the loan: (i) the originating bank (Penn Square) up to its legal limit, and (ii) a correspondent bank (e.g. Continental Illinois National

---

[25]Zweig [58], p. 82
[26]Zweig [58], p. 68

Bank and Trust Company) with a much larger maximum loan cap who lent the remainder of the loan's notional. The bank that originates the loan (in this case Penn Square Bank) receives an origination fee, usually 1/2 to 1 % of the loan's notional value[27].

Assessing the value of the underlying collateral for oil and gas mortgage loans is a difficult task. Indeed, the value of the oil and gas leases requires estimates of the reserves in the ground which is difficult to determine before drilling, especially for deep-well natural gas leases. And, even after drilling occurs, the value of the well and the efficiency of the drilling operation takes a long time to evaluate[28]. This ambiguity allowed subjective judgment to be applied in the determination of the quality of the loan's collateral and consequently the loan's credit risk.

Apparently, in some cases Penn Square Bank issued the letters of credit to itself[29]. This, of course, is equivalent to Penn Square Bank having to assume the loan if the loan fails which is equivalent to this asset disappearing from the balance sheet from the perspective of Penn Square Bank (except the bank receives the initial option premium).

15.2.3 Market Risk

The credit risk of the oil and gas mortgage loans directly depends on the market prices of oil and natural gas, especially deep-well gas (greater than 15,000 feet in ground). This is the embedded market risk. Penn Square Bank's activities of lending helped to create a price bubble in the underlying collateral.

In addition, the cost of Penn Square Bank's funding (certificates of deposit and demand deposits) depend on the evolution of the term structure of interest rates. This is an additional market risk in Penn Square Bank's balance sheet.

15.2.4 Credit Risk

The credit risk of the oil and gas mortgage loans is directly related to the value of the loan's underlying collateral. As noted above, the values of the underlying collateral - the oil and gas leases - were subjective in their determination and easily manipulated by the bank's loan officers to justify the issuance of credit risky loans.

---

[27] Zweig [58], p. 81
[28] Zweig [58], p. 57
[29] Zweig [58], p. 87, 191

15.2.5 Liquidity Risk

Penn Square Bank had two sources of liquidity risk.

Funding Risk

Funding risk is common to banks. Penn Square Bank funded much of its loan portfolio with CDs. This generates funding risk because unlike ordinary demand deposits which are long-term in duration (because they are provided by ordinary individuals and insured by the FDIC up to $100 thousand at this time), large CDs are uninsured (if greater than $100 thousand) and can be (easily) withdrawn from a bank by not rolling them over. This is called a *bank run*.

Funding risk is the conjunction of liquidity risk and binding borrowing constraints. If markets were perfectly liquid, Penn Square Bank could sell assets to meet CD and demand deposit withdrawals. However, the selling of illiquid assets causes the value of the bank's remaining assets' to decline more (due to the quantity impact of selling on the price). This makes increased deposit withdrawals more likely. This downward spiral does not solve the cash flow crisis.

Loan Impact on Lease and Partnership Share Prices

Penn Square Bank's lending activities had a quantity impact on the underlying oil and gas lease and partnership share prices. The market prices of the leases and partnership shares (in turn) affected the market for energy loans, increasing the demand for such loans, which (in turn) increased Penn Square Bank's (paper) profits. This is a manipulative trading strategy that facilitated the creation of a price bubble in oil and gas leases.

15.2.6 Operational Risk

Penn Square Bank faced significant operational risk in the assessment of the quality of the oil and gas mortgage loans. As noted above, determining the "true" value of the underlying collateral was a subjective exercise and these values were easily manipulated by the loan officers. In addition, the loan approval and documentation process was not properly monitored at Penn Square Bank by the board of directors[30].

---

[30] Zweig [58], Chapter 25

15.3   Conclusion

The reasons for Penn Square Bank's failure are well documented. The management team at Penn Square Bank was incompetent, fraudulent, and they issued loans for personal gains (personal promotion within the bank, personal cash flows, to benefit friends, etc.) as opposed to the quality of the loans. This abuse was facilitated by poor oversight of Penn Square Bank's management by the bank's board of directors.

In summary:

1. Penn Square Bank's excessive lending helped to create a price bubble in oil and gas leases and equity partnership shares. This story illustrates an interesting example of investing/lending in such a market climate and the losses that can occur.

2. The root cause of the bank's failure was operational risk because of inadequate risk management controls on the bank's loan portfolio.

Chapter 16

Metallgesellschaft (1993)

This Chapter is based on Culp and Miller [13, 14], Edwards and Canter [16], and Mello and Parsons [51].

16.1 Summary

Metallgelsellschaft (MG), A.G. was a German industrial conglomerate located in Frankfurt, Germany that supplied raw materials, engineering, and financial services. In 1994 it was the 14th largest company in Germany. In 1993 MG's total sales exceeded 26 billion (Deutsch marks) DM, its assets equalled 17.8 billion DM, and it employed 43,292 individuals.

In 1993 an oil futures trading strategy lost the company an equivalent of 1.3 billion U.S. dollars. The management board at the MG subsidiary (MG Refining and Marketing) that was responsible for this trading strategy was fired and the company avoided bankruptcy only through a bailout in 1994 consisting of 1.9 billion U.S. dollars from a consortium of 150 international banks. The DM/$ exchange rate was approximately 1.6 at this time.

The background for the losses were as follows.

1. The company *sold* forward contracts on gasoline, diesel fuel, and heating oil for either 5 or 10 years into the future to its customers. Most of the contracts were for 10 years (see Mello and Parsons [51], p. 107). These were long-dated fixed price contracts. This was due to MG's marketing program. In September 1993, MG had sold forward approximately 160 million barrels of petroleum products. As a note, these contracts contained an embedded option that allowed the customer to terminate the contract early if market prices increased, presumably protecting the customers for credit risk if the customers

141

thought that MB would not be able to fulfill the contracts. The details of this embedded option can be found in Culp and Miller [13]. These contracts controlled counter party risk by limiting the contract size to any customer to 20% of the customer's needs (see Mello and Parsons [51], p. 107).

2. In an attempt to hedge the market price risks, MG *purchased* short-term oil futures contracts, rolling over the positions as the futures contracts matured. These contracts were one to three month futures traded on the New York Mercantile Exchange (NYMEX) with the underlying commodities being either New York harbor regular unleaded gasoline, New York harbor No. 2 heating oil, or West Texas Intermediate (WTI) grade light sweet crude oil. The futures position was for approximately 55 million bbl. These were among the most liquid petroleum contracts traded on NYMEX. MG also purchased commodity swaps in the OTC derivatives market for about 105 million bbl. MG's swap contracts paid fixed and received floating payments based on energy prices. These swap contracts were all short-term in maturity (mostly 3 months or less). The hedge ratios used for both the futures and swap contracts were unity (one). This is an important fact to remember in the subsequent analysis. Together, the total longs were about 160 million bbl, which equalled the total shorts (a hedge ratio of unity).

Energy prices dropped significantly in late 1993. For example, crude oil dropped from $19 per barrel in June to below $15 in December. This resulted in the following changes in the trading strategy's value.

1. The fixed price forward contracts increased in value, but since they were forwards, the change in value generated no cash inflows or outflows. These contracts were with customers and without collateral or margin restrictions.

2. The futures contracts lost value. Due to marking-to-market (daily settlement), the losses generated a cash outflow on the futures positions as margin calls needed to be satisfied. These negative cash flows were enormous. The OTC derivative contracts also lost value and more collateral would also have been requested to guarantee these positions. The total capital required to be posted to meet these funding demands was around $900 million (see Edwards and Canter [16], p. 97).

To meet these margin and collateral calls, MG needed to employ other financing sources: either borrow cash, liquidate assets, or close out its futures and OTC derivative positions. MG did not use any of these alternative funding sources. Perhaps no reasonable funding alternatives were available, although Edwards and Canter [16], p. 102 argue that this is not the case. A counter argument is given in Mello and Parsons [51], p. 110. Instead, MG's management board decided to liquidate its futures position (terminate the futures hedge). No details on the treatment of its OTC derivative positions is available.

MG also reduced the size of its customers' forward contracts. The exact magnitude of this reduction is unavailable. Note that MG reduced the size of its forward contract position because this naked position (without the hedge) generated significant market price risk on its balance sheet.

A bank bailout followed to cover the resulting losses and presumably MG's OTC derivative collateral needs. The company was restructured. MG eventually recovered and became profitable again. MB is now part of the GEA Group, A.G.

16.2 The Trading Strategy

This section describes the trading strategy in a simplified fashion to highlight the economics of the hedging strategy.

Time horizon $[0, T]$.

Spot price of commodity S_t.

Forward price $K(0, \tau)$ for delivery date τ.

Futures price $k(0, \tau)$ for delivery date τ.

The simplified trading strategy is as follows.

1. A short position in one forward contact on spot S_t with delivery date T and forward price $K(0, T)$. This is a *long-term* contract.

2. A long position in n_0 futures contracts on spot S_t with delivery date $\tau \ll T$ and futures price $k(0, \tau)$. Let $c \cdot \tau = T$ where $c > 1$ is an integer. At time τ when the futures expires, a long position in n_τ futures contracts on spot S_t with delivery date 2τ and futures price $k(\tau, 2\tau)$ is taken. At time 2τ when the futures expires, a long position in $n_{2\tau}$ futures contracts on spot S_t with delivery date 3τ and futures price $k(2\tau, 3\tau)$ is taken. This strategy is continued until time T. This is a hedging strategy based on *short-term* futures contracts.

In the implementation of its futures trading, MG set the hedge ratio $n_t = 1$ for all t.

Based on the models in Part III, the following is a list of the relevant risks involved in the trading strategy.

16.2.1 Market Risk

Note that there are three issues to be studied in the correctness of this hedging strategy:

(i) complete or incomplete markets,
(ii) forward versus futures contracts, and
(iii) long-term versus short-term contracts.

These simplify to the following two questions:

(a) are markets complete, and if so
(b) were the correct $n_0, n_\tau, \ldots, n_{(c-1)\tau}$ chosen to construct a perfect hedge?

At present and during this time period, due to the trading of futures contracts and swaps, the market for petroleum products was approximately complete. Hence, the question reduces to choosing the correct hedge ratios. In this regard, an exact hedge could have been obtained if a proper model was used. To account for the differences between forward and futures contracts, stochastic interest rates need to be included. This is easily handled by the HJM model in Chapter 4. This model was not used, although it existed at the time. To account for the maturity mismatch due to using short-term futures to hedge long-term forwards, a multiple-factor model for the term structure of futures prices analogous to that used in the HJM model in Chapter 4 is required. Such a model needs multiple futures to hedge the forward contract's value. This model was also not used, although it existed at the time. Instead, Metallgesellschaft used a single futures to hedge the forward contracts with the hedge ratio equalling unity.

16.2.2 Credit Risk

Credit risk is not a direct issue in this trading strategy. Margin accounts for exchange traded futures and collateral requirements for OTC derivatives mitigated credit risk to MG.

16.2.3 Liquidity Risk

This hedging strategy is subject to liquidity risk.

(i) The forward contract position is illiquid and generates no cash flows. Being contracts with customers for physical delivery, no collateral agreements analogous to those in OTC derivative contracts existed.

(ii) The futures contract position is liquid, but it is subject to cash flows (marking-to-market) in the futures margin account. In addition, the OTC derivatives position is illiquid and subject to the posting of additional collateral. If the futures and OTC derivatives positions lost significant value, a cash flow crisis could occur. This is funding risk, which is the conjunction of liquidity risk and binding margin requirements. If markets were otherwise perfectly liquid, MG could have sold assets to meet its margin requirements. But, in this case the assets were illiquid. Sales would have only generated increased losses on its balance sheet, not solving a cash flow crisis.

16.2.4   Operational Risk

The operational risk existing to the extent that MG's management incorrectly: (i) determined the market risk of the hedging strategy, and (ii) accounted for the funding risk.

16.3   Conclusion

The reasons for MG's losses are debated in the literature. Culp and Miller [13] argue that the hedging strategy was correct, but that liquidity risk was mismanaged. Edwards and Canter [16] argue that the hedging strategy was partially correct, and that funding risk was the cause of the failure. They make no judgements concerning mismanagement, leaving open the possibility that the event was just "bad luck." In contrast, Mello and Parsons [51] argue that funding risk was mismanaged and that the hedging strategy was incorrect.

The evidence supports the conclusions of Mello and Parsons [51]. In summary:

1) Market risk was not correctly hedged due to the use of incorrect models to capture both the maturity mismatch and the difference between forward and futures contracts. MG used a hedge ratio equal to unity. This is certainly not correct. An empirical paper supporting this assertion is Pirrong [55].

2) Funding risk was not properly anticipated by the management team.

Chapter 17

Orange County (1994)

The reference for this Chapter is Jorion [46].

17.1 Summary

Orange County is a municipality in southern California. In 1993, its GDP was larger than that of Portugal. Orange County collects taxes from its citizens and it receives investment funds from various public utilities (e.g. water and sanitation), school districts, and local municipalities within its jurisdiction. The investment funds received include pension fund contributions. These cash proceeds are accumulated in the Orange County Investment Pool (OCIP). The OCIP invests these funds to finance the future operations of Orange County and the respective public utilities and local municipalities. From a money management perspective, the public utilities and local municipalities are investors in the OCIP.

The OCIP invested its capital in various investment grade fixed income securities including agency bonds, certificates of deposit, mortgage backed securities, corporate bonds, and mutual funds[1]. In 1994, prior to the investment loss, the OCIP equalled \$7.5 billion dollars. Notable in the OCIP was their investments in agency bonds, the majority of which were *inverse floaters* (defined in Chapter 2). Also notable is that the OCIP partially levered its investment portfolio using reverse repurchase agreements (explained in Chapter 2). Orange County issued municipal bonds to finance its operations. The outstanding principal on these bonds totaled almost

---

[1] Jorion [46], p. 81

147

1.8 billion dollars during February 1995[2]. OCIP's leverage ratio was 1.5 in June 1990 and it increased to 2.7 by November 1994[3].

In 1994, the OCIP was managed by the Orange County treasurer-tax collector Robert Citron. This is an elected position. Citron had held this position for approximately 24 years. Prior to 1994, Citron's investment performance was unusually good. Citron's average yearly return was 8-9%, compared to the California Treasurer's average return of only 5-6%. This performance received national attention. Due to Citron's successful investment performance, he was able to avoid independent audits of his activities[4], and he was able to convince the California legislature to allow Orange County and other municipalities to invest in various interest rate derivatives (e.g. reverse repurchase agreements). In addition, his exception performance led to a lack of monitoring of his activities by Orange County's Board of Supervisors.

Much of Citron's successful investment performance occurred during a period of continually declining interest rates from 1989 - 1993[5]. Rates fell during this period from around 10% to 3%. Citron's successful investment strategy was based on speculating that interest rates would be stable or falling. In February 1994, the Federal Reserve Board initiated a monetary policy of increasing interest rates. Interest rates increased rapidly from 3% in 1993 to between 5 and 6% by mid-1994.

Because of Citron's leverage and speculative position, by November 1994 (roughly 8 months), the OCIP lost 1.6 billion dollars. This was a 22.3% loss[6]. These large losses resulted in Orange County going bankrupt. Orange County went bankrupt because of funding risk. First, when the losses were announced, various local municipalities wanted to withdraw their funds from the OCIP. This created a run on the OCIP, similar to a bank run. Second, due to the OCIP's use of reverse repurchase agreements, the OCIP received margin calls from various investment banks requiring more collateral to be posted as the value of the original collateral declined. Because its investments in fixed income securities were illiquid, it could not sell its holdings to meet the cash flow demands from its clients or margin calls without a significant negative impact on the value of the remaining assets due to liquidity risk. Orange County declared bankruptcy on December 6, 1994. Citron was forced to resign his position. He pleaded guilty to fraud charges and was sentenced to a year in prison plus a $100,000 fine.[7] The bankruptcy proceedings generated legal costs and necessitated the eventual

[2]Jorion [46], p. 110
[3]Jorion [46], p. 88
[4]Jorion [46], p. 11
[5]Jorion [46], p. 86
[6]Jorion [46], p. 82
[7]http://www.nytimes.com/1997/10/25/business/ex-treasurer-freed-in-california-county.html

liquidation of the OCIP fund resulting in the losses quoted earlier. The liquidation costs were significant, estimated to be over \$100 million dollars[8].

17.2 The Trading Strategy

This section describes the trading strategy in a simplified fashion to highlight the economics involved. The OCIP used fixed income securities to speculate on the future evolution of interest rates. The OCIP's trading strategy speculated that interest rates would be stable or declining in the future. The OCIP trading strategy consisted of three components: (i) investments in long-term coupon bonds, (ii) investments in inverse floaters, and (iii) leverage via the use of reverse repurchase agreements. The fixed income securities included in its portfolio contained minimal credit risk.

17.2.1 Long-term Coupon Bonds

The OCIP invested in long-term coupon bonds that were nearly default-free. For the purposes of this analysis, we assume that they are default-free (e.g. U.S. Treasuries). Consider a default-free coupon bond with coupon rate c, maturity date τ, and a face value 1 dollar with coupon payments at times $t = 1, \ldots, T$. Its time t price is denoted $\mathfrak{B}(t, \tau)$ for $0 \leq t \leq \tau \leq T$. From Chapter 13 we know that the value of a coupon bond can be written as

$$\mathfrak{B}(t, \tau) = \sum_{i=t+1}^{\tau-1} cP(t, i) + (c+1)P(t, \tau)$$

where $P(t, T)$ is the price of a default-free zero-coupon bond at time t with maturity T.

Let r_t be the default-free spot rate of interest. Using the HJM model of Chapter 4, it can be shown that as the spot rate increases, $P(t, T)$ declines, and so does $\mathfrak{B}(t, \tau)$. Consequently, an investment in a coupon bond is a bet that interest rates will stay stable or decline. Usually, the longer the maturity of the coupon bond, the larger is the bond's sensitivity to changes in interest rates (this can be seen using the notion of a bond's duration). Hence, the longer the maturity of the coupon bond, the more risky is the bet on stable or declining interest rates.

---

[8] Jorion [46], p. 106

17.2.2   Inverse Floaters

An inverse floater is a fixed income security with a maturity date τ, a notional of 1 dollar (without loss of generality), and a coupon rate of c. Its coupon payments are reduced as an underlying floating rate increases (this is the inverse floating aspect). As shown in Chapter 13, an inverse floater can be shown to be equivalent to a portfolio consisting of a coupon bond, shorting a floating rate bond, long a zero-coupon bond, and long an interest rate cap. Indeed, no arbitrage implies that

$$\mathfrak{C}_0 = \mathfrak{B}(0, \tau) - 1 + Cap_0 + P(0, \tau)$$

where $\mathfrak{C}_0$ is the time 0 value of the inverse floater, $\mathfrak{B}(0, \tau)$ is the time 0 value of the coupon bond, the floating rate bond is always valued at par (1 dollar), Cap_0 is the time 0 value of the cap, and $P(0, \tau)$ is the time 0 value of a zero-coupon bond with maturity τ.

Let r_t be the default-free spot rate of interest. As the spot rate increases, the inverse floater's value declines. This can be seen by noting that as the spot rate increases: (i) the coupon bond values declines (shown above), (ii) the floating rate bond's value stays constant at a dollar, (iv) the zero-coupon bond's value declines, and (iv) the interest rate cap's value increases. However, the increase in the cap's value does not offset the losses on the coupon bond and the zero-coupon bond. This is because the cap's delta to changes the interest rate is less than the sum of the deltas of the remaining components. Consequently, purchasing an inverse floater is a bet on stable or declining interest rates.

17.2.3   Leveraging via Reverse Repurchase Agreements

The OCIP used reverse repurchase agreements to lever its bond portfolio. The economics of this transaction were discussed in Chapter 2. For easy reference, we repeat the argument here. Leveraging via reverse repurchase agreements takes place in the following manner.

1. Buy a bond.

2. Borrow the value of the bond using the bond as collateral (this is the reverse repurchase agreement).

3. Take the cash obtained from the borrowing and purchase a second bond. This generates a leverage ratio of 2.

4. Next, borrow the value of the second bond using the second bond as collateral (this is a second reverse repurchase agreement).

5. Take the cash obtained from the second borrowing and purchase a third bond. This gives a leverage ratio of 3.

6. Continue this process to obtain the desired leverage ratio.

OCIP used this trading strategy to obtain a leverage ratio between 1.5 in June 1990 to 2.7 in November 1994[9].

The Mathematics of Leveraging

This section explains how leveraging increases the risk of an investment portfolio.

Let C_t be the capital invested at time t.
Let α represent the investment in fixed income securities S_t at time t.
Let B_t be the dollars borrowed at the rate r at time t.
Then, an accounting identity gives:

$$C_t = \alpha S_t - B_t.$$

The percentage of the portfolio in the securities S_t is $w = \frac{\alpha S_t}{C_t} > 1$ and the percentage of the portfolio in borrowings is $1 - w = -\frac{B_t}{C_t} < 0$.
The return on the capital over $[t, t + \triangle t]$ is determined as follows:

$$C_{t+\triangle} = \alpha S_{t+\triangle} - (1 + r)B_t,$$

$$\frac{C_{t+\triangle} - C_t}{C_t} = \frac{\alpha S_t}{C_t}\left(\frac{S_{t+\triangle} - S_t}{S_t}\right) - \frac{B_t}{C_t}r = w\left(\frac{S_{t+\triangle} - S_t}{S_t}\right) + (1-w)r.$$

Letting $R_C = \frac{C_{t+\triangle} - C_t}{C_t}$ and $R_S = \frac{S_{t+\triangle} - S_t}{S_t}$, we have in return form:

$$R_C = wR_S + (1-w)r.$$

Note that
$$E_t(R_C) = wE_t(R_S) + (1-w)r, \text{ and}$$
$$\sqrt{Var_t}(R_C) = w\sqrt{Var_t}(R_S)$$

where $Var_t(\cdot)$ is the variance computed at time t.
The leverage ratio in this trading strategy is $\frac{B_t}{C_t} = -(1-w)$.
Consequently, the return on the fixed income securities is multiplied by $w = 1 + \frac{B_t}{C_t} > 1$. For example, if OCIP's average leverage ratio was 2, then the expected return and standard deviation of the spread was multiplied by a factor of 3. To illustrate, if $E_t(R_S) = .05$, then $wE_t(R_S) = 3(.05) = .15$. This completes the explanation.

---

[9] Jorion [46], p. 88

17.2.4   Market Risk

The trading strategy was subject to significant market risk because it was speculating on stable or declining interest rates.

17.2.5   Credit Risk

The trading strategy had minimal credit risk in its investment portfolio. The credit risk was minimized by their investing in investment grade corporate and agency bonds. With respect to their reverse repurchase agreement positions, there was minimal counter party risk from their investment bank counter parties due to the financial stability of the investment banks.

17.2.6   Liquidity Risk

Due to the leveraging, the trading strategy was subject to liquidity risk in two forms.

(i) A "run on the fund" could occur if there is bad news and clients request their funds to be returned. Liquidating a large portion of the fund's investments to return investor capital was costly due to the liquidity risk in holding illiquid fixed income securities.

(ii) The reverse repurchase agreement positions were subject to the posting of additional collateral if the value of the original collateral declined significantly. This is funding risk, which is the conjunction of liquidity risk and binding collateral requirements. To post more collateral, OCIP needed to sell assets, but the quantity impact of selling caused its remaining assets' values to decline further, requiring more collateral to be posted. This created a downward spiral, which eventually led to Orange County's bankruptcy.

17.2.7   Operational Risk

The operational risk existing in this trading strategy was in OCIP's management incorrectly: (i) predicting interest rate movements and (ii) accounting for the funding risk.

17.3   Conclusion

The evidence is that OCIP's losses were due to a speculative investment strategy followed by OCIP's investment fund manager. Additional losses were incurred by management's neglect of funding risk in the event of a substantial loss on the OCIP portfolio. The evidence supports the contention that OCIP's management did not understand the risk of their investment strategy.

Chapter 18

Barings Bank (1995)

The reference for this Chapter is Fay [18].

18.1 Summary

Barings Bank was started in 1762 in London, England by Francis Baring. As a financial institution, it had a long and glorious history. Its ownership and control remained with the Baring family until its failure in February 1995. Its failure was caused by a rogue trader, Nick Leeson, who joined the bank in 1989. In 1992, Leeson was transferred to Singapore to run their futures trading group. He had a dual responsibility for managing both the trading and settlement processes. This dual responsibility enabled Leeson to fraudulently manipulate the profits and losses of various accounts without adequate monitoring by the senior management at Barings Bank.

This inadequate monitoring of Leeson's trading activities was due to the organizational structure at Barings, and the newness of the Singapore branch of Barings Bank, called Barings Futures (Singapore) Ltd, which was started in 1992. Leeson obtained an agreement to obtain unlimited and unmonitored access to Barings Bank's capital to meet the margin calls of Barings Bank's clients[1]. This unrestricted access to capital was crucial to the size of the losses that Leeson accumulated. In addition, the Singapore International Monetary Exchange (SIMEX) waved position limits on Barings Singapore's trading activities[2] and Barings Bank imposed no internal position limits as well[3]. This was also key to the size of losses that

---

[1]Fay [18], p. 98
[2]Fay [18], p. 92
[3]Fay [18], p. 127

Leeson accumulated. If either of these restrictions had been in place, the size of Leeson's losses would have been capped and, perhaps, the bank's failure might have been avoided.

Leeson was able to trade and distort profits and losses by the use of an "error trading account" number 88888, to which he deposited all trading losses, thereby showing only positive profits in visible accounts. To generate some profits, he performed front-running of his clients' positions[4]. Front-running occurs when a broker, knowing his client's order to buy, buys for his own account first at a lower price and then sells to his client at a higher price, pocketing the difference (a broker can also front-run a short sale as well). Front-running is illegal in most countries.

Leeson traded options and futures on the Nikkei 225 index[5]. The Nikkei 225 is a price weighted index of 225 stocks traded on the Tokyo Stock Exchange. Between 1992 and 1995, Leeson accumulated losses equalling 869 million pounds[6], which exceeded Barings Bank's capital, causing the bank to fail[7]. The precipitating event for the large losses was a severe earthquake in Kobe, Japan on January 17, 1995. The earthquake resulted in the Nikkei 225 index falling dramatically in a short time period. When the Nikkei 225 declined, Leeson had a long position in Nikkei 225 futures, a short option straddle on the Nikkei 225 index, and a short position in Japanese government bonds. All of these positions lost significant value[8].

Leeson was tried for fraudulent activities, pleaded guilty, and was sentenced to 6.5 years in a Singapore jail[9].

18.2   The Trading Strategy

This section describes the trading strategy in a simplified fashion to highlight the economics involved. Leeson's trading strategy consisted of two major components: naked futures and option straddles. He also shorted Japanese government bonds[10].

18.2.1   Naked Futures

Leeson had authority to do "statistical arbitrage (stat arb)," which is trading mispricings between the Nikkei 225 futures prices and the Nikkei 225 Index

---

[4]Fay [18], p. 136
[5]Fay [18], p. 92, 141
[6]Fay [18], p. 1
[7]Fay [18], Chapter 11
[8]Fay [18], p. 154
[9]Fay [18], p. 3
[10]Fay [18], p. 154

spot prices[11]. We first describe stat arb between spot and forward prices on the Nikkei 225 index. Following this discussion, we analyze the impact of replacing futures with forward contracts in the trading strategy.

Recall from Chapter 13 the cost of carry argument for synthetically constructing a forward contract using the underlying spot asset and shorting zero-coupon bonds. Initially, we ignore the dividends paid on the stocks in the index and market frictions (transaction costs and trading constraints).

Let S_t be the time t price of the Nikkei 225 index.

Consider a forward contract on the Nikkei 225 index with delivery date τ and forward price $K(0, \tau)$. The payoff to the forward contract at the delivery date τ is:

$$[S_\tau - K(0, \tau)].$$

To synthetically construct this forward contract's payoffs, buy the underlying Nikkei 225 index at time 0 and short $K(0, \tau)$ default-free zero-coupon bonds maturing at time τ. Buying the Nikkei 225 index means buying the stocks in the Nikkei 225 index in the same proportions as represented in the index. We note that this is a costly activity.

The payoff to this portfolio at time τ is:

$$[S_\tau - K(0, \tau)].$$

To avoid arbitrage the cost of constructing this portfolio at time 0 must be zero (because the cost of entering a forward contract is zero). Hence,

$$K(0, \tau)P(0, \tau) = S_t.$$

This expression relates the forward price of the Nikkei 225 index to the spot price of the Nikkei 225 index itself (the value of the underlying portfolio).

The stat arb trading strategy is as follows:

(i) If $K(0, \tau)P(0, \tau) > S_t$, then sell the forward and synthetically construct a long position in the forward with the synthetic forward price $\frac{S_t}{P(0,\tau)}$. Pocket the difference in the initial costs of forming the strategy, and note that there is no future liability since the long and short positions exactly offset each other. This is an arbitrage opportunity under the above qualifications.

(i) If $K(0, \tau)P(0, \tau) < S_t$, then buy the forward and synthetically construct a short position in the forward. Pocket the difference in the initial costs of forming the strategy, and note that there is no future liability since the long and short positions exactly offset each other. This is an arbitrage opportunity under the above qualifications.

In practice, this trading strategy needs to be adjusted for dividends and market frictions. The short or long position in the Nikkei 225 index

---
[11]Fay [18], p. 106, 122

must account for the dividends paid. And, the costs of buying and selling the 225 stocks underlying the Nikkei 225 index needs to be included. These adjustments are easily accommodated (see Jarrow and Chatterjea [37], Chapter 12).

As noted earlier, this stat arb trading strategy exploits mispricings between forward contracts and positions in the spot index. In practice, forward contracts are replaced by futures contracts since forward contracts are not traded in liquid markets. Using futures contracts instead of forward contracts in this trading strategy introduces additional risk due to the marking-to-market (daily settlement) of futures contracts. This difference makes the stat arb trading strategy not a "true arbitrage."

Leeson did not do both legs of the stat arb trading strategy, but instead only speculated on movements of the Nikkei 225 Index using long positions in the futures alone[12]. Employing only one leg of the arbitrage strategy implies the trading strategy was speculative.

18.2.2 Option Straddles

To obtain cash flows to finance his margin accounts, Leeson sold option straddles on the Nikkei 225 index. An option straddle is a position short both a call and put option on the index. To understand this position, we introduce some notation.

Let S_t be the time t price of the Nikkei 225 index.

Consider a European call with maturity date τ and a strike price K_c on the Nikkei 225 index.

The call option's payoff is:

$$max[S_\tau - K_c, 0].$$

Let $\mathcal{C}_0$ be the call's time 0 value.

Consider a European put with maturity date τ and a strike price K_p on the Nikkei 225 index.

The put option's payoff is:

$$max[K_p - S_\tau, 0].$$

Let $\mathcal{P}_0$ be the put's time 0 value.

A short option straddle is to sell the call and to sell the put with strike prices $K_c > S_0 > K_p$.

---

[12]Fay [18], p. 175

The time τ payoff to the trading strategy is

$$\text{short straddle}_\tau = \begin{cases} -[S_\tau - K_c] & \text{if} & S_\tau > K_c \\ 0 & \text{if} & K_c \geq S_\tau \geq K_p \\ -[K_c - S_\tau] & \text{if} & K_p > S_\tau. \end{cases}$$

The short straddle generates a positive time 0 cash flow equal to:

$$\mathcal{C}_0 + \mathcal{P}_0.$$

As shown, this trading strategy benefits if the index stays with the range $K_c \geq S_\tau \geq K_p$, it generates losses if the index is otherwise (and exceeds the initial premiums).

In addition, Leeson recognized that he had a quantity impact on the price of options[13] and futures[14]. Selling decreases the price of the option (perhaps the underlying index as well). Since Leeson was short options, the option's prices declined as he sold more options. This decreased the value of his liability (short positions), generating paper profits. Such a trading strategy required continued selling, so that the quantity impact did not dissipate. The same economic argument applies to trading futures as well.

18.2.3 Market Risk

Leeson's trading strategy was subject to significant market risk. The trading strategy was speculating on the evolution of the Nikkei 225 index price. Since Leeson also shorted Japanese government bonds, he was also exposed to interest rate risk.

18.2.4 Credit Risk

The trading strategy had minimal credit risk in that the trades were executed on SIMEX. The risk of the exchange defaulting was negligible.

18.2.5 Liquidity Risk

The trading strategy was subject to liquidity risk in three forms.

1. The futures position was subject to margin calls. Margin calls imply funding risk. Funding risk is the conjunction of liquidity risk and the margin requirements being binding. Indeed, if markets were perfectly liquid, Barings could have sold assets to meet its margin call. Here,

---

[13]Fay [18], p. 142 - 144
[14]Fay [18], p. 225

however, selling assets caused more marked-to-market losses because the sales lowered the value of its remaining assets. Additional margin calls resulted. This downward spiral eventually caused Barings Bank's failure.

2. The option position's profits depended on a temporary quantity impact on the price due to his massive trading of options. When Leeson stopped selling, his option positions lost value.

3. Leeson had a massive position in Nikkei 225 futures. When liquidated quickly, the value of this position diminished considerably (this occurred when SIMEX liquidated Barings Bank's futures position).

18.2.6   Operational Risk

Operational risk to the bank existed because the trading strategy was not adequately monitored by senior management. This occurred for two reasons. One, Leeson managed both the trading and settlement process, hence he could manipulate the observed profits via this joint responsibility. Two, his access to capital was unrestricted and not monitored. This enabled Leeson to accumulate large losses, directly reducing Barings Bank's capital.

18.3   Conclusion

The losses to Barings Bank were due to inadequate risk management controls and a fraudulent trader. Senior management did not understand the source of Leeson's positive returns.

Chapter 19

Long Term Capital Management (1998)

The references for this Chapter are Lowenstein [50], Edwards [17], and Jorion [47].

19.1   Summary

Long Term Capital Management (LTCM) was a hedge fund created in 1994 by a group of former Solomon Brothers' bond traders and quantitatively inclined academics, most of whom had a strong connection to the Massachusetts Institute of Technology (MIT). The initial capital in the fund was $1.3 billion. LTCM was a quantitative hedge fund. Their management fee was 2% of capital plus 25% of profits, which was higher than the norm of 1% and 20%. Their primary trading strategy was betting on the mean-reversion of various spreads, based on historical relationships. They traded on spreads across different fixed income securities: bonds (governments, private), mortgage backed securities; and to a lesser extent spreads across different equities. Using options, they also placed speculative bets that the market's volatility was mean reverting (see Lowenstein [50], p. 234). Because their trading strategies could lose value before finally generating profits, investors in LTCM were required to lock-up their invested funds for three years.

A key component of their trading strategy was leverage. Based on the convergence of abnormal spreads, their trading strategies generated small (but positive) expected profits. To increase the magnitude of their returns, they highly levered their positions. A typical leverage ratio was 25 to 1

161

(see Jorion [47], Fig. 3). The majority of their financing was done using repurchase agreements and interest rate swaps. Increasing leverage typically increases the variance of a portfolio. LTCM allegedly controlled the portfolio's variance using diversification and quantitative methods based on historical correlations in market prices.

In the beginning LTCM was very successful. From 1994 - 1997 their returns were (after fees) 19.9%, 42.8%, 40.8%, 17.1%, respectively. Capital under management increased to $7 billion by 1997. Problems started in the spring and summer of 1997. In the spring of 1997, mortgage-backed securities prices declined, causing a 16% loss to LTCM's capital. In August 1997, Russia defaulted on is debt, causing LTCM's cumulative capital loss to reach 52%. These losses dramatically increased LTCM's leverage ratio, increasing the severity and magnitude of additional shocks to its capital.

As LTCM lost capital, it received margin and collateral calls on its exchange traded and OTC positions. To fulfill these calls, it liquidated its assets. As it liquidated its assets, the quantity impacts from the trades caused prices to fall further, cascading and accelerating the loss in the value of its positions. This is funding risk. By September 1998 only $400 million in LTCM's capital remained. LTCM was on the verge of failure. LTCM reached out to private investors for additional capital, but negotiations failed.

LTCM's continued forced liquidations, in conjunction with the market turmoil caused by the Russian debt default, created the possibility of a financial market failure. To avoid such a calamity, on September 23rd the New York Federal Reserve organized a bailout of LTCM consisting of a $3.6 billion capital infusion by 14 banks for a 90% position in the firm (see Jorion [47], p. 283). The bailout avoided a market failure. In early 1999 LTCM was dissolved and the bailout investors departed earning a reasonable return on their capital.

19.2   The Trading Strategy

This section describes the trading strategy in a simplified fashion to highlight the economics involved.

Let X_t and Y_t denote the market prices of two closely related assets (e.g. a government and corporate bond of 10 years to maturity).

Let $S_t = X_t - Y_t$ be the spread in market prices. Although spreads are normally described in terms of yields, for simplicity (and without loss of generality), we illustrate the trading strategy with price spreads.

Suppose that based on historical relationships, the spread satisfies the following evolution over the time interval $[t, t + \Delta t]$:

$$\triangle S_t = \kappa(\mu - S_t)\triangle t + \triangle M_t$$

where $\kappa > 0$, $\mu > 0$, $\Delta M_t = M_{t+\Delta t} - M_t$, and M_t is a martingale (hence, $E_t(\triangle M_t) = 0$).

This implies that the spread S_t follows a mean-reverting process with its long-term value equal to μ. The expected change in the spread is:

$$E_t(\triangle S_t) = \kappa(\mu - S_t)\triangle t.$$

If $S_t > \mu$, then S_t is expected to decline. If $S_t < \mu$, then S_t is expected to increase.

The trading strategy consists of three steps. Step 1 is the spread position, step 2 is the leveraging, and step 3 is diversification.

19.2.1   Step 1 (The Spread Trade)

1. If $S_t > \mu$, then sell the spread, i.e. sell X_t and buy Y_t. Hold this position until $S_t = \mu$, then liquidate. At this time either X_t will have declined, Y_t will have increased, or both will have occurred generating a profit.

2. If $S_t < \mu$, then buy the spread, i.e. buy X_t and sell Y_t. Hold this position until $S_t = \mu$, then liquidate. At this time either X_t will have increased, Y_t will have decreased, or both will have occurred generating a profit.

Note that this is not an arbitrage opportunity because there is a positive probability that the spread may never converge, due to the random component $\triangle M_t$. It is also important to observe that the trading strategy can lose value before convergence occurs. Hence, the ability to fund the losses must be part of the trading strategy.

19.2.2   Step 2 (The Leveraging)

This section explains how leveraging increases the risk of an investment portfolio.

Let C_t be the capital invested at time t.

Let α represent the shares in the spread trade S_t at time t.

Let B_t be the dollars borrowed at the rate r at time t.

Then, an accounting identity gives:

$$C_t = \alpha S_t - B_t.$$

The percentage of the portfolio in the spread S_t is $w = \frac{\alpha S_t}{C_t} > 1$ and the percentage of the portfolio in borrowings is $1 - w = -\frac{B_t}{C_t} < 0$.

The return on the capital over $[t, t + \triangle t]$ is determined as follows:

$$C_{t+\triangle} = \alpha S_{t+\triangle} - (1+r)B_t,$$

$$\frac{C_{t+\triangle} - C_t}{C_t} = \frac{\alpha S_t}{C_t}\left(\frac{S_{t+\triangle} - S_t}{S_t}\right) - \frac{B_t}{C_t}r = w\left(\frac{S_{t+\triangle} - S_t}{S_t}\right) + (1-w)r.$$

Letting $R_C = \frac{C_{t+\triangle} - C_t}{C_t}$ and $R_S = \frac{S_{t+\triangle} - S_t}{S_t}$, we have in return form:

$$R_C = wR_S + (1-w)r.$$

Note that

$$E_t(R_C) = wE_t(R_S) + (1-w)r, \text{ and}$$
$$\sqrt{Var_t}(R_C) = w\sqrt{Var_t}(R_S)$$

where $Var_t(\cdot)$ is the variance computed at time t.

The leverage ratio in this trading strategy is $\frac{B_t}{C_t} = -(1-w)$. Consequently, the return on the spread is multiplied by $w = 1 + \frac{B_t}{C_t} > 1$. For example, if LTCM's average leverage ratio was 25, then the expected return and standard deviation of the spread was multiplied by a factor of 26. To illustrate, if $E_t(R_S) = .001$, then $wE_t(R_S) = 26(.001) = .026$.

19.2.3 Step 3 (Diversification)

To reduce the variance of the balance sheet, LTCM diversified its position by investing in a collection of spreads $S_1, \ldots, S_n$.

The return on the spread portfolio is

$$R_C = \sum_{j=1}^{n} w_j R_{S_j} + (1-w)r$$

where

$$w \equiv \sum_{j=1}^{n} w_j > 1.$$

LTCM choose $(w_1, \ldots, w_n)$ such that the variance of the portfolio was set to equal that of the market portfolio, i.e.

$$Var_t(R_C) = \sum_{i=1}^{n}\sum_{j=1}^{n} w_i w_j cov_t(R_{S_i}, R_{S_j}) = \sigma_{market}^2$$

where σ_{market}^2 is the variance of the equity market portfolio.

19.2.4 Market Risk

This trading strategy is subject to the price risks inherent in the evolution of the spreads.

19.2.5 Credit Risk

The trading strategy used fixed income securities, some of which could default. Credit risk was a component of LTCM's trading strategy.

19.2.6 Liquidity Risk

First, since the trading strategy involved buying and selling assets when spreads deviated from their norms, liquidity risk played a role in the profits earned. Indeed, spreads often deviate from their norms when markets are less liquid than typical. Second, using a highly levered trading strategy, a "cash flow crisis" occurred due to funding risk, which is the conjunction of liquidity risk and borrowing constraints being binding. Indeed, when LTCM sold assets to cover margin and collateral calls, the impact of the sales caused more marked-to-market losses, generating additional margin calls. Borrowing constraints were binding, inhibiting the ability to obtain outside funding without selling assets. This cash flow crisis only stopped when a bailout plan was created, which provided outside funding.

19.2.7 Operational Risk

The operational risk existed in this hedging strategy to the extent that LTCM's management incorrectly: (i) determined the market and credit risk and (ii) accounted for funding risk.

19.3 Conclusion

It has been argued by LTCM's management that their methodology was correct, but they suffered from extreme bad luck in the occurrence of a 3.7 sigma event in their market and credit risk exposures (see Jorion [47], p. 289). Others disagree with this conclusion. For example, Jorion [47], p. 287 argues that LTCM did not adequately take into account changing asset correlations across healthy and distressed markets. There seems to be no debate that LTCM did not understand or adequately account for liquidity risk and binding borrowing/margin requirements - funding risk - in their risk management procedures.

In summary, the evidence support's the following:

1) Market and credit risk were not correctly modeled by LTCM.

2) Funding risk was not properly anticipated by the management team.

Chapter 20

The Credit Crisis (2007)

The references for this Chapter are Lewis [49], Crouhy, Jarrow, Turnbull [12], and Jarrow [33]. Studying the 2007 credit crisis is important because it illustrates the economy wide risks encountered in risk management of a firm's or individual's balance sheet.

20.1 Summary

The genesis of the credit crisis was a healthy U. S. economy in the late 1990s and early 2000s with a nation-wide sustained growth in residential home values, now widely believed to have been a price bubble. In conjunction, interest rates were low from a historical perspective in the early 2000s and the equity market was in the midst of a sustained bull market. We argue below that the financial markets prior to 2007 were in the midst of an economy-wide Ponzi scheme, based on the continued growth in housing prices. When the alleged housing price bubble burst, the Ponzi scheme collapsed. This collapse was the 2007 credit crisis.

20.1.1 The Ponzi Scheme

The housing price expansion was fueled, in fact, accelerated by an enormous supply of capital available for home mortgages, especially to low income households. This capital was available from two sources: (i) government agencies (Fannie Mae and Freddie Mac), and (ii) financial institutions: commercial banks, investment banks, hedge funds, mutual funds, insurance companies, and pension funds. It was available from government agencies partly because of government legislation promoting an increase

167

in the supply of low income home mortgages (e.g. the American Dream Downpayment Act of 2003). It was available from financial institutions because they sought high yields on "nearly riskless" fixed income securities in an otherwise low interest rate environment. Within these financial institutions, the money managers' compensation schemes, especially bonuses, were short-term oriented. These short-term incentives influenced these investment decisions.

To generate these "nearly riskless" fixed income securities with high yields, structured products and credit derivatives were created by investment banks and hedge funds. These structured products were asset backed securities (ABS) with home loans as the collateral pool, collateralized debt obligations (CDOs) with ABS as the collateral pool, and credit default swaps (CDS), see Chapter 2 for a description of these securities. The issuance of these credit derivatives experienced exponential growth prior to the crisis.

It is costly to create such structured products. They were created because an arbitrage opportunity existed in their issuance, due to these structured products being misrated by the credit rating agencies (Moodys, Standard and Poor's (S&P), and Fitch Investor Services, among others). These misratings were partly due to the perverse incentives created by the manner in which rating agencies are paid for their services. The rating agencies are paid by the entities requesting the ratings for their fixed income securities (including structured products). Favorable ratings to a client facilitated the issuance of the client's fixed income securities, thereby generating more and continuing business for the rating agencies.

These misratings implied that the structured products were not nearly riskless, and they were overvalued by the market. Unfortunately, this fact was not understood by the vast majority of the financial institutions. We note that the entities creating the structured products did so to take advantage of this *rating arbitrage* opportunity. The money managers within the financial institutions did not perform their own due diligence for the simple reason that the structured products were complex financial derivatives, difficult to model and to understand. Their short-term based compensation schemes reinforced these decisions. Consequently, the money managers within financial institutions delegated this aspect of their risk management responsibility to the credit rating agencies.

In the creation and use of these structured products, CDS were essential. CDS are term insurance contracts written to insure against the default of ABS and CDOs. The sellers of CDS, therefore, guarantee payment in the event of default. To guarantee payment on these CDS, the sellers must maintain collateral, formalized in the CDS contract's master agreements. Unfortunately, due to the networking of collateral across the economy and the lack of transparency in this networking, the collateral underlying the CDS was not sufficient to guarantee payments in the event of massive defaults. This also was not understood by the majority of the participants in the OTC derivative markets at the time.

20.1.2 The Collapse

The economy-wide Ponzi scheme collapsed because the supply of new home owners disappeared. This occurred for two reasons. First, the low-income families desiring homes became depleted. Second, interest rates increased due to the Iraq war making the financing of new home mortgages and the maintaining of existing home mortgages beyond the means of the low income households. Consequently, low income households began to default on their home mortgages. This was a nation-wide phenomena. These defaults, in turn, caused defaults on the structured products - the ABS and CDOs. These defaults, in turn, caused defaults on CDS because the sellers did not have sufficient capital to fulfill their obligations. Numerous financial and non-financial institutions failed or were bailed out by the U. S. federal government. The U. S. Treasury implemented the Troubled Asset Relief Program (TARP) to provide emergency funding for commercial banks. The collapse of the financial markets caused equity markets to collapse, and the start of the Great Recession.

20.2 The Trading Strategy

To illustrate the risks faced by a financial institution in the credit crisis, we consider a generic financial institution and three simplified trading strategies.

20.2.1 Buying ABS and CDOs

The first trading strategy is to buy ABS or CDOs. Examples of failed financial institutions following this strategy were Bear Stearns and Merill Lynch.

Market Risk Since ABS and CDOs are fixed income securities, these securities are subject to interest rate risk. Indirectly, since the risk of housing prices affects the behavior of the households in the underlying mortgage loan collateral pools, the risk of home prices is also relevant to this trading strategy, but only to the extent that it affects mortgage default and the securities' credit risk.

Credit Risk   ABS and CDOs contain credit risk because the promised payments on these securities may not be paid in the event of large-scale home owner defaults.

Liquidity Risk   ABS and CDOs contain substantial liquidity risk because they trade in over-the-counter (OTC) market, which is a market between banks and large financial institutions (as contrasted with a trading exchange). In times of financial stress, there would be a substantial quantity impact on the price from trading.

Operational Risk   ABS and CDOs are complex credit derivatives that contain many embedded options. There is significant operational risk if the management do not understand derivative technology and delegate this responsibility to the credit rating agencies. In addition, money managers are typically short-term oriented due to their compensation schemes. This implies that they benefit from the upside of risky investments, but if they "blow-up" the financial institution, they do not incur the extreme losses. They can seek employment elsewhere.

20.2.2   Buying CDS

This second trading strategy is to buy CDS to insure against default of an ABS or CDOs. An example of a financial institution that experienced significant losses due to this strategy was the Canadian Imperial Bank of Canada (CIBC).

Market Risk   Indirect, to the extent that the counter party's ability to pay off on the CDS depends on market risk.

Credit Risk   CDS are insuring the credit risk of the ABS and CDOs. CDS also bear the risk that the counter party to the CDS contract (the seller) will pay off on the insurance in the event of default. The CDS master agreement collateral provisions are included to mitigate this risk.

Liquidity Risk   CDS contain substantial liquidity risk because they trade in OTC markets. In times of financial stress, there would be a substantial quantity impact on the price from trading.

Operational Risk   It is difficult to estimate the probability of an ABS or CDOs defaulting and the resulting recovery rate. There is significant operational risk if the management do not understand derivative technology and delegate this responsibility to the credit rating agencies.

20.2.3   Selling CDS

The third trading strategy is to sell CDS to provide insurance against default of an ABS or CDOs. An example of a financial institution that experienced significant losses due to this strategy was American International Group (AIG).

Market Risk   Indirect, to the extent that the default of an ABS or CDO depends on market risk.

Credit Risk   CDS are insuring the credit risk of the ABS and CDOs. The seller faces minimal counter party risk from the buyer of the CDS.

Liquidity Risk   CDS contain substantial liquidity risk because they trade in OTC markets. In times of financial stress, there would be a substantial quantity impact on the price from trading.

Operational Risk   It is difficult to estimate the probability of an ABS or CDOs defaulting and the resulting recovery rate. There is significant operational risk if the management do not understand derivative technology and delegate this responsibility to the credit rating agencies.

20.3   Conclusion

The evidence supports the conclusion that the major reason for the failures of most financial institutions was due to operational risk in the inability of the money managers to understand the risk of the structured products and CDS held in their portfolios. This mismanagement of balance sheet risk also included a mis-assessment of the counter party credit risk and the liquidity risk present in these OTC derivatives. Prior to 2007, the derivatives methodology for understanding and managing these risks was available. The reasons for their non-use were commented on above. We note that there were a few players (hedge funds) who exploited this methodology to their advantage prior, during, and after the crisis.

Chapter 21

Washington Mutual (2008)

The reference for this Chapter is Grind [21].

21.1 Summary

Washington Mutual (WaMu) was a savings and loan (S&L) located in Seattle, Washington. The story of WaMu's failure begins with the appointment of Kerry Killinger as President of WaMu (later becoming Chairman of the Board) in December 1988. At that time, WaMu had assets of $7 billion[1]. Killinger expanded WaMu's size through an ambitious and aggressive strategy of acquiring related financial institutions across the United States. By 1998, after the purchase of H.F. Ahmanson in California (the country's largest S&L at the time[2]), WaMu became the seventh-largest financial institution in the U.S. with approximately 2,000 branches and $150 billion in assets[3]. In 2008, before its failure, WaMu assets totaled $310 billion[4].

In the mid-90s and early 2000s, the U.S. government pursued a policy of increasing homeownership, especially for low income and minority families. This, in conjunction with rising residential housing prices, lead to a boom in financial institutions providing home mortgages to credit risky individuals, called subprime mortgages[5]. The increased capital available for home loans, in turn (a feedback loop), lead to an increase in housing prices, and has been argued to create a housing price bubble (see Chapter 20).

---

[1] Grind [21], p. 30
[2] Grind [21], p. 40
[3] Grind [21], p. 54
[4] Grind [21], p. 246
[5] Grind [21], p. 64, 122

WaMu's entry into this market started with the purchase of Long Beach Financial in 1999[6], and continued in the early 2000s with internal growth and the purchases of PNC Financial Services Group, Bank United, Fleet Mortgage Company, and Dime Bancorp[7]. By 2003 WaMu was the largest S&L in the country with $268 billion in assets and with over 3,000 branches across the U.S.[8].

Over the period 1999-2008, WaMu invested in and originated an enormous quantity of home equity loans and adjustable rate mortgages, called Option ARMs. By March 2008, WaMu had accumulated on its balance sheet $60 billion in home equity loans and $58 billion in Option ARMs[9]. The incentives within the bank were such that the employees were compensated on the quantity of the loans issued, and not their quality. This lead to the issuance of subprime loans without adequate documentation or with fraudulent documentation. 90 percent of WaMu's home equity loans[10] and 75 percent of their Option ARMs were without adequate documentation[11].

A significant quantity of WaMu's mortgage loans were issued to borrowers who could not repay the loans if economic conditions worsened or housing prices declined[12]. This was because the Option ARMs had embedded options that enabled the borrower to pay low floating rates in the beginning of the loan's life (teaser rates) often for 2 or 3 years. In addition, these loans also allowed the borrower to postpone a percent of the floating payments until later in the loan's life when a cap on the principal was reached (negative amortization). These low initial rates were purposefully designed to be affordable to low income households. And, when the terms of the loans caused these low interest payments to be increased, as long as housing prices were rising, the borrowers could refinance with the increased home equity value to maintain the lower rates.

WaMu's loan originations helped to finance the housing price bubble. The housing bubble burst in mid-2006, when home prices started to decline[13]. The reasons for this decline are briefly discussed in Chapter 20. This decline in home prices eventually caused massive defaults in WaMu's subprime mortgage portfolio. For example, in the fall of 2007, WaMu's bad loans alone totaled $5.5 billion[14]. In the fourth quarter of 2007, the

---

[6]Grind [21], p. 63
[7]Grind [21], p. 85
[8]Grind [21], p. 88
[9]Grind [21], p. 232
[10]Grind [21], p. 126
[11]Grind [21], p. 186
[12]Grind [21], p. 139 -145
[13]Grind [21], p. 151
[14]Grind [21], p. 170

first and second quarter of 2008 home mortgage defaults lead to WaMu's reporting losses of $1.9 billion, $1 billion, and $3.3 billion, respectively[15].

WaMu experienced a bank run of $16.7 billion dollars in mid to late September 2008[16], generating a funding crisis, due to its reported losses and the deteriorating conditions in financial markets. On September 25, 2008 the OCC (Office of the Comptroller of the Currency) declared the bank insolvent, the FDIC took receivership of the bank, and the bank was sold to JPMorgan[17]. WaMu's equity holders, debt holders, and subordinated debt holders lost their entire values in the sale[18]. No depositors lost money[19].

21.2 The Trading Strategy

This section describes the trading strategy in a simplified fashion to highlight the economics involved. WaMu invested heavily in subprime mortgages, Option ARMs and home equity loans. Home equity loans can be 2nd mortgages on the equity appreciation in a home's equity value above a 1st mortgage's value. WaMu's trading strategy speculated on the performance of these home mortgages.

21.2.1 Option ARMs

An Option ARM is a floating rate loan with a residential home as collateral. The loan has a maturity date (often 30 years) and a principal. The "ARM" means that the interest rate payments adjust (float) with an interest rate index (usually related to Treasury rates or a bank's cost of funds). The loan can be "hybrid" where the rate is fixed for the first 2 or 3 years, and floating thereafter. These are initial teaser rates making the loans attractive to low income borrowers because refinancing is possible at future dates.

Normal floating rate loans require monthly payments equal to the interest payment plus an amortization of the principal. The "Option" means that the floating rate loan has three embedded options with respect to the monthly payments: (i) pay the required payment amount *or more* to reduce the maturity of the loan, (ii) pay the required interest payment only and none of the principal, or (iii) pay a minimal amount (below the floating interest rate) adding the omitted interest to the principal until a cap on the principal is reached, then paying the required payment amount (interest plus amortization of the principal) thereafter[20].

---

[15]Grind [21], p. 185, 244
[16]Grind [21], p. 304
[17]Grind [21], p. 303
[18]Grind [21], p. 7
[19]Grind [21], p. 305
[20]Grind [21], p. 112

21.2.2   Market Risk

The credit risk of home mortgages, especially the Option ARMs, directly depend on the market prices of residential homes. In addition, the cost of WaMu's funding (certificates of deposit and demand deposits) depend on the evolution of the term structure of interest rates. This is an additional market risk on WaMu's balance sheet. WaMu was apparently aware of this interest rate risk and partially hedged it by issuing these ARM's[21].

21.2.3   Credit Risk

The credit risk of home mortgages is directly related to the value of the home and the borrower's ability to make interest payments. As noted above, a low income family's ability to make interest payments was often conditional upon continually increasing home prices and an ability to refinance the loan.

21.2.4   Liquidity Risk

As a bank, WaMu had funding risk. WaMu funded its assets with borrowings (deposits and CDs) and equity. Funding risk is the conjunction of liquidity risk and binding borrowing constraints. In liquid markets, WaMu could sell assets or continue to borrow funds using the marked-to-market value of its assets as collateral. But with liquidity risk, selling assets causes the value of the remaining assets to decline (due to the quantity impact on the price from selling), causing more losses. This in turn causes more deposit withdrawals. Borrowing additional funds is impossible because borrowing constraints are binding in financial distress.

21.2.5   Operational Risk

WaMu faced significant operational risk in the issuance of home mortgage loans. As noted above, the incentives for issuing loans were based on quantity and not quality.

21.3   Conclusion

The reasons for WaMu's failure are rooted in their asset growth strategy based on issuing mortgages with fraudulent or inadequate documentation to borrowers who could not afford the interest payments if housing prices declined.

---

[21]Grind [21], p. 122

In summary:

1. WaMu's excessive lending helped to create a price bubble in home prices.

2. WaMu purposefully speculated in its loan portfolio on housing prices. Its lending affected the prices of the underlying collateral for its loans, increasing its (paper) profits. This story illustrates an example of (unintended) price manipulation.

3. When housing prices declined, funding risk created a cash flow crisis. The bank's failure was due to operational risk because of inadequate risk management controls on the bank's issuance of poor quality mortgage loans.

Bibliography

[1] K. Amin and R. Jarrow, 1992, Pricing options on risky assets in a stochastic interest rate economy, *Mathematical Finance*, 2 (4), 217 - 237.

[2] R. Ash, 1972, *Real Analysis and Probability*, Academic Press, New York.

[3] K. Back, 2010, *Asset Pricing and Portfolio Choice Theory*, Oxford University Press, U.K.

[4] N. Barberis and R. Thaler, 2003, A survey of behavioral finance, *Handbook of Economics and Finance*, Vol. 1, Part B, Financial Markets and Asset Pricing, eds. G. Constantinides, M. Harris, R. Stulz, Elsevier B.V.

[5] F. Black and M. Scholes, 1973, The pricing of options and corporate liabilities, *Journal of Political Economy*, 81, 637 - 659.

[6] S. Boyd and L. Vandenberghe, 2004, *Convex Optimization*, Cambridge University Press, U. K.

[7] Brealey, R., S. Myers, F. Allen, 2011, *Principles of Corporate Finance*, McGraw Hill, N.Y.

[8] M. Broadie, J. Cvitanic, and H. Soner, 1998, Optimal replication of contingent claims under portfolio constraints, *Review of Financial Studies*, 11 (1), 59 - 79.

[9] P. Carr and D. Madan, 2002, Towards a theory of volatility trading, working paper, University of Maryland.

[10] U. Cetin, R. Jarrow and P. Protter, 2004, Liquidity risk and arbitrage pricing theory, *Finance and Stochastics*, 8 (3), 311 - 341.

[11] U. Cetin, H. Soner, and N. Touzi, 2010, Option hedging for small investors under liquidity costs, *Finance and Stochastics*, 14, 317 - 341.

[12] M. Crouhy, R. Jarrow, S. Turnbull, 2008, The subprime credit crisis of 2007, *Journal of Derivatives*, Fall, 81 - 110.

[13] C. Culp and M. Miller, 1995, Metallgesellschaft and the economics of synthetic storage, *Journal of Applied Corporate Finance*, 7 (4), 62 - 76.

[14] C. Culp and M. Miller, 1995, Hedging in the theory of corporate finance: a reply to our critics, *Journal of Applied Corporate Finance*, 8 (1), 121 - 127.

[15] F. Delbaen and W. Schachermayer, 1998, The fundamental theorem of asset pricing for unbounded stochastic processes, *Mathematische Annalen*, 312, 215 - 250.

[16] F. Edwards and M. Canter, 1995, The collapse of Metallgesellschaft: unhedgeable risks, poor hedging strategy, or just bad luck?, *Journal of Applied Corporate Finance*, 8 (1), 86 - 105.

[17] F. Edwards, 1999, Hedge funds and the collapse of Long Term Capital Management, *Journal of Economic Perspectives*, 13 (2), 189 - 210.

[18] S. Fay, 1996, *The Collapse of Barings,* W. W. Norton & Co., New York.

[19] Federal Deposit Insurance Corporation, 1998, *Managing the Crisis: The FDIC and RTC Experience 1980-1984*, FDIC, Washington D.C.

[20] P. Glasserman, 2003, *Monte Carlo Methods in Financial Engineering*, Springer, New York.

[21] K. Grind, 2012, *The Lost Bank: the story of Washington Mutual - the biggest bank failure in American History*, Simon & Schuster, New York.

[22] J. Harrison and S. Pliska, 1981, Martingales and stochastic integrals in the theory of continuous trading, *Stochastic Processes and their Applications*, 11, 215 - 260.

[23] D. Heath, D., R. Jarrow and A. Morton, 1992, Bond pricing and the term structure of interest rates: a new methodology for contingent claims valuation, *Econometrica*, 60 (1), 77 - 105.

[24] R. Jarrow, 1987, An integrated axiomatic approach to the existence of ordinal and cardinal utility functions, *Theory and Decision*, 22, 99 - 110.

[25] R. Jarrow, 1992, Market manipulation, bubbles, corners, and short squeezes, *Journal of Financial and Quantitative Analysis*, 27 (3), 311 - 336.

[26] R. Jarrow, 1994, Derivative security markets, market manipulation, and option pricing theory, *Journal of Financial and Quantitative Analysis*, 29 (2), 241 - 261.

[27] R. Jarrow, 2002, Put option premiums and coherent risk measures, *Mathematical Finance*, 12 (2), 135 - 142.

[28] R. Jarrow, 2008, Operational risk, *Journal of Banking and Finance*, 32, 870 - 879.

[29] R. Jarrow, 2009, The term structure of interest rates, *Annual Review of Financial Economics*, 1, 69 - 96.

[30] R. Jarrow, 2009, Credit risk models, *Annual Review of Financial Economics*, 1, 37 - 68.

[31] R. Jarrow, 2010, Active portfolio management and positive alphas: fact or fantasy?, *Journal of Portfolio Management*, Summer, 17 - 22.

[32] R. Jarrow, 2012, The third fundamental theorem of asset pricing, *Annals of Financial Economics*, 7 (2), 11.

[33] R. Jarrow, 2012, The role of ABS, CDS and CDOs in the credit crisis and the economy," *Rethinking the Financial Crisis*, eds., A. Blinder, A. Lo, and R. Solow, Russell Sage Foundation.

[34] R. Jarrow, 2015, Bubbles and multiple-factor asset pricing models," forthcoming, *International Journal of Theoretical and Applied Finance*.

[35] R. Jarrow, 2016, An equilibrium CAPM in markets with trading constraints and price bubbles, working paper, Cornell University.

[36] R. Jarrow, 2016, *Continuous Time Asset Pricing Theory: a Martingale Based Approach*, lecture notes, Cornell University.

[37] R. Jarrow and A. Chatterjea, 2013, *An Introduction to Derivative Securities, Financial Markets, and Risk Management*, W. W. Norton and Co., New York.

[38] R. Jarrow and M. Larsson, 2012, The meaning of market efficiency, *Mathematical Finance*, 22 (1), 1 - 30.

[39] R. Jarrow, J. Oxman, and Y. Yildirim, 2010, The cost of operational risk loss insurance, *Review of Derivatives Research*, 13, 273 - 295.

[40] R. Jarrow and P. Protter, 2016, Positive alphas and a generalized multiple-factor asset pricing model, *Mathematics and Financial Economics*, 10 (1), 29 - 48.

[41] R. Jarrow and A. Purnanandam, 2007, The valuation of a firm's investment opportunities: a reduced form credit risk perspective, *Review of Derivatives Research*, 10, 39 - 58.

[42] R. Jarrow and P. Protter, 2008, An introduction to financial asset pricing, *Handbooks in OR & MS*, (15), eds., J. R. Birge and V. Linetsky, Elsevier B.V.

[43] R. Jarrow and P. Protter, 2010, The martingale theory of bubbles: implications for the valuation of derivatives and detecting bubbles, *The Financial Crisis: Debating the Origins, Outcomes, and Lessons of the Greatest Economic Event of Our Lifetime*, ed., Arthur Berd, Risk Publications.

[44] R. Jarrow and S. Turnbull, 1992, Credit risk: drawing the analogy, *Risk Magazine*, 5 (9).

[45] R. Jarrow and S. Turnbull, 1995, Pricing derivatives on financial securities subject to credit risk, *Journal of Finance*, 50 (1), 53 - 85.

[46] P. Jorion, 1995, *Big Bets Gone Bad: Derivatives and Bankruptcy in Orange County*, Academic Press, San Diego, CA.

[47] P. Jorion, 2000, Risk management lessons from Long Term Capital management, *European Financial Management*, 6 (3), 277 - 300.

[48] P. Jorion, 2001, *Value at Risk*, 2nd edition, McGraw Hill, N.Y.

[49] M. Lewis, 2011, *The Big Short: Inside the Doomsday Machine*, W.W. Norton & Co.

[50] R. Lowenstein, 2000, *When Genius Failed: The Rise and Fall of Long-term Capital Management*, Random House, N. Y.

[51] A. Mello and J. Parsons, 1995, Maturity structure of a hedge matters: lessons from the Metallgesellschaft debacle, *Journal of Applied Corporate Finance*, 8 (1), 106 - 120.

[52] R. C. Merton, 1973, Theory of rational option pricing, *Bell Journal of Economics*, 4 (1), 141–183.

[53] W. Schachermayer, 2001, Portfolio optimization in incomplete financial markets, *Mathematical Finance: Bachelier Congress 2000*, eds., H. Geman, D. Madan, S. R. Pliska, T. Vorst, Springer, 427 - 462.

[54] H. Pham, 2009, *Continuous time Stochastic Control and Optimization with Financial Applications*, Springer.

[55] S. Pirrong, 1997, Metallgesellschaft: a prudent hedger ruined, or a wildcatter on NYMEX?, *Journal of Futures Markets*, 17 (5), 543 - 578.

[56] P. Protter, 2005, *Stochastic Integration and Differential Equations*, Second Edition, Version 2.1, Springer.

[57] W. Rudin, 1976, *Principles of Mathematical Analysis*, 3rd edition, McGraw Hill, New York.

[58] P. Zweig, 1985, *Belly Up: the collapse of the Penn Square Bank*, Gawcett Columbine, New York.

Index